WE THE PEOPLE ARE THE PROBLEM

How Americans Betrayed America

PETER MAGISTRALE

Copyright © 2020 by Peter Magistrale

All rights reserved. No part of this book may be reproduced or used in any matter without written permission of the copyright owner except for the use of quotations in a book review.

ISBN: 9798656102612 (paperback)

Table of Contents

Preface		v
1	Our Civic Duties	1
2	How the Wealthy Betrayed America	7
	Public School: A Weapon of the Rulers	8
	Siphoning the Nation's Wealth	29
	War and Terrorism	31
	Propaganda	41
	Fascism in America	47
	The Enlightened Wealthy	65
3	The Middle Class Indictment	70
	Culture and Values	70
	Ignorance Has Real Consequences	74
	Blind Loyalty to Political Parties	79
	American Society is Based on Ignorance	81
	Civic Duty and COVID-19	84
	True Patriotism	86
	Equality is a Myth	87
	Ruler's Education	88
	An Enlightened Culture	90
	Taxing Civic Ignorance	92
	The Cost of Ignorance	98
	Middle Class Heroes	101

4	What Americans Can Learn from Ancient Rome	104
	The Virtue of Appius Claudius	104
	The Virtue of Gaius Fabricus Luscinus	106
	Roman Virtue During the First Punic War	107
5	Historic Civic Failures	110
	The French Revolution	111
	The Russian Revolution	118
6	How We Can Live Up to Our Civic Duty	127
	Petrarca	128
	Cicero	129
	José Ortega y Gasset	134
	Plato	143
	Death as Motivation	148
	Malcolm X	153
	Conclusion	155
Works Cited		157

Preface

It is a dream of mine to see Americans turn away from the vain and vacuous world built for them and toward the truth, toward the pursuit of their potential, and toward the advancement of mankind. My ultimate aim is to see my fellow citizens reject the cave of ignorance and set out on a path informed by truth, motivated by purpose, and guided by duty.

The motivation to write this book came from my experience running for the New York State Senate in 2016. I decided to run for office under the assumption that if the corrupt could be removed from power then the government could actually solve problems. Running for office made me see something that may have taken decades to learn otherwise. The corrupt were empowered by everyday people who were blinded by misplaced loyalty and willful ignorance. In short, the corrupt were empowered by people who had lost their sense of civic duty.

I'm an accountant. I didn't go to an Ivy League college. I come from a family of Sicilian immigrants who left Sicily in the 1970s because Sicily was ruled by the iron fist of the Mafia and offered no future to honest people. Relative to Sicily, America was a meritocracy, where ability and hard work were the drivers of success. My grandfather, whom I'm named after, was a farmer in Sicily but a farmer with four girls. He came to

America in his fifties and sacrificed everything he had built to provide a better life for his daughters. My mother left Sicily at fifteen, graduated from college, and had a successful career in banking. Had she stayed in Sicily, her life would've been extraordinarily different. Millions of other people have similar stories—stories of how America saved them and their families from poverty, war, and hopelessness.

Make no mistake. America is a special place, a place worth fighting for, and a place that the human race depends on. There are elements of this book that are harsh, including indictments of treasured American institutions and American culture. The purpose of these discordant elements is to find the root cause of America's decline and reverse it because if America falls humanity will be thrown into a certain dark age. Don't take America for granted. As Americans, we are stewards of the most powerful nation on earth. Humanity depends on us, and we cannot let it down.

The structure of the book is straightforward.

Chapter 1 outlines our civic duties.

Chapters 2 and 3 are devoted to the civic crimes committed by the wealthy and middle class against America.

Chapter 4 focuses on what Americans can learn from the civic virtue of the early Roman Republic.

Chapter 5 dives into two momentous revolutions that failed due to the unenlightened actions of everyday people.

Lastly, chapter 6 draws on the inspiration of Cicero, Plato, and others to help the reader live up to their civic duties.

1

OUR CIVIC DUTIES

In the final days of the Roman Republic, the great republican martyr and Roman statesman, Cicero, may well have reflected on who brought down the republic. If he walked the Roman streets, he would find the guilty and possibly ponder a devastating thought:

> "Do not blame Caesar, blame the people of Rome who have so enthusiastically acclaimed and adored him and rejoiced in their loss of freedom and danced in his path and gave him triumphal processions. Blame the people who hail him when he speaks in the Forum of the 'new, wonderful good society' which shall now be Rome, interpreted to mean 'more money, more ease, more security, more living fatly at the expense of the industrious.'"[1]

As Americans, we are the modern-day guardians of mankind's greatest assets and aspirations. We have the power to push humanity into a 1,000-year dark age or into the heavens of an unprecedented enlightenment. We have the privilege of freedom because of the great acts of previous generations who first threw off the chains of royal despotism, then righted the wrong of slavery, and finally helped liberate the world from fascism. Our lives are more enriched because of the accumulated contributions of millions of Americans who came before us. Millions of people the world over, from Europe to South Korea, would be living under the rule of dictators today if it weren't for the courageous acts of our ancestors.

The only way America will remain a force for human progress is if the American people value truth, fulfill their civic duty, and reserve apathy for the superficial things in life. To be worthy of this great inheritance, we must protect America by living up to our civic duty.

Our civic duties include removing corrupt politicians from public office, making rationally informed voting decisions, understanding the law-making process, and relinquishing blind loyalty associated with partisanship.

Our civic duties are born out of our values. It's impossible to fulfill our duties as citizens unless we value truth more than comfort, sustainability over short-term gratification, and excellence over mediocrity. The more we lose touch with reality, the more we long for instant gratification, and the more we accept the status quo, the more likely the corrupt will rule, high crimes will go unpunished, and America will serve unenlightened ends.

To fulfill these duties, we must understand the political arena, the characters, and the rules. We need to understand that the most important aspects of our lives, such as free movement, free association, and free speech, can be destroyed by a malevolent government empowered by ignorant citizens. Every country has demagogues, sociopaths, and pathological liars. It's our civic duty to ensure that people with these qualities never occupy positions of power in our government. Far too many Americans are derelict in their civic duties. We have elevated the worst among us into positions of power, we are enslaved by confirmation bias, and we are experts in triviality but wholly illiterate in public affairs. Our consumer culture is superficial, our politicians are corrupt parasites, and our economy has left millions behind in the name of limitless profits.

Extremism rules our politics. The Republican Party has been hijacked by the Alt Right and gravitated to nativism, jingoism, and authoritarianism. The Democratic Party has drifted left, embracing gender politics, socialism, and championing entitlement over personal responsibility.

Who is responsible for the debasement of America? We the People are 100% responsible.

Only when we understand that we are the problem will we take personal responsibility and focus on how we can improve and strengthen our republic. The message of this book is tough love because it indicts Americans from all socioeconomic backgrounds for not doing enough to protect our society from the many forms of corruption, but it is done out of a genuine desire to see Americans live up to their highest potential.

Fortune has bestowed countless blessings on America, including two vast oceans protecting its coasts, internal waterways helping to improve logistics, the climate and land needed to feed the entire nation without depending on food imports, vast natural resources, plentiful drinking water, and a relatively moderate climate. These natural gifts were then multiplied by the man-made gifts of the Founding Fathers. Far from perfect but nonetheless exceptional, the Founding Fathers set in motion the unleashing of vast human potential that would lead to world-changing inventions: the Hubble Space Telescope, global positioning system (GPS), magnetic resonance imaging machine (MRI), the Internet, personal computers, cellphones, Wi-Fi, and email are some of the most notable.

All of these natural and man-made gifts have aided America's ascent from thirteen colonies to world superpower and given you the opportunity to use technology a few generations before could only dream of. You are living in the most technologically advanced time in human history.

The sword of progress has another side though. With each step up the mountain of progress, the risks get more catastrophic, and wisdom becomes a necessity, not a luxury.

Too many of us forget that freedom requires responsibility. We want the convenience of modern life without the responsibility of protecting it. Civilization is far more vulnerable than we realize because we have recency bias. We project in the future what we've most recently experienced. Of all the nations the world over, the United States is the most important when it comes to determining the future of the human race. This places monumental importance on the American people. There is a place for entertainment, but there must be a much larger place for the acquisition of knowledge that makes us more informed and more productive citizens. Knowledge is what secures our posterity—knowledge of ourselves, knowledge of justice, and

We The People Are The Problem

knowledge of human affairs. Without knowledge, we are not much above beasts, and without wisdom, knowledge is meaningless. How each of us thinks and acts is of supreme importance.

The first step in solving a problem is caring enough to contribute to the solution. If your best friend had suddenly started doing cocaine and getting in trouble with the law, how would you try to help him? Would you tell him he's perfect, doesn't need to change, and join in the hedonistic revelry? In effect, this is what politicians do when they pander to voters. A decent person would focus on helping their troubled friend reverse course so that they wouldn't destroy their life. Likewise, thoughtful citizens understand that they will need to take a more active role in public life to address the fundamental issues facing our country. I implore all people of goodwill and sound judgment to step out into the public arena and contribute to America's enlightened rebirth.

Another thing that impedes solutions is blaming public problems on groups, political parties, or specific leaders instead of taking personal responsibility for at least a portion of the problem. We must not be tempted to look for scapegoats. Do not blame the Republican Party, the Democratic Party, or any specific politician, as they are all symptoms of our national disease. The disease itself resides in the soul of Americans. Rich and poor alike have rejected truth, civic duty, and our republic's foundational principles.[2] This disease rots the soul of our nation by multiplying illusions, destroying civic responsibility, and promoting narcissism.

Some people would say that all those corrupt politicians or corrupt corporate executives are responsible for America's decline. They do bear responsibility, but they aren't the cause. Who elects those politicians in Congress that everyone despises and who buys the products sold by corrupt corporations? It is the American people who give power to the corrupt. How could Congress have an approval rating below 25%[3] but a reelection rate above 90%? It's because we the people have failed to protect our republic from the ignorant, the greedy, and the corrupt. If republican democracy is to survive in America, it must have more enlightened citizens.

There are many factors that contribute to a democratic nation's success, but none is more important than the quality of its citizens. Citizen competency is absolutely critical. Citizens must be able and willing to make informed decisions regarding the most important issues of their society. They must be capable of holding leaders who are incompetent or corrupt accountable, either by voting them out or seeking legal action. They must be able and willing to seek the truth of public and private events that affect public policy. Most importantly, they must not let propaganda, national myths, or a love of ease inhibit their duties as citizens.

> "Congress has an approval rating of 25% and a reelection rate above 90%." Who is responsible for that?

"The greatest crimes in humanity occur when power and ignorance combine."

2

HOW THE WEALTHY BETRAYED AMERICA

What crimes are the wealthy guilty of committing against our republic?

They are the most culpable of all, but before we enumerate their crimes, let's first understand human nature. The greatest shortcoming of humanity is the misuse of power. The greatest crimes in human history occur when power and ignorance combine in unholy matrimony. The wealthy, by definition, have enormous power, but the vast majority lack the wisdom to use their power justly. It's very important to understand that the middle class and poor would commit the same crimes if given the opportunity.

We cannot be naïve to think that an enlightened world can spring from the ashes of the rich. An enlightened world can only spring from enlightened people. Enlightened people put truth before ignorance, their love of human progress over their love of power, and their love of excellence and achievement

7

over entertainment and ease. Can we honestly say that any sizable portion of American society has those qualities? If we are honest, the answer is no. We must first enlighten Americans.

The crimes listed below are intended to show the profoundly unenlightened actions of the wealthy, but before your rage has you thinking of a guillotine, remember that the middle class and poor are equally unenlightened, and a revolution before their enlightenment would be a human disaster.

Here are some of the most consequential crimes the wealthy have committed against our republic:

- Creating a public school system to produce passive, obedient, and ignorant people, who are easy to rule
- Siphoning the nation's wealth with corporate welfare and out-of-control defense spending
- Taking the nation to war based on lies to advance their economic and political objectives
- Hollowing out America's soul by using propaganda to make people consumer shopaholics devoid of any purpose in life except accumulating status symbols

PUBLIC SCHOOL: A WEAPON OF THE RULERS

> "Let us go back and distinguish between the two things that we want to do; for we want to do two things in modern society. We want one class of persons to have a liberal education, and we want another class of persons, a very much larger class, of necessity, in every society, to forego the privileges of a liberal education

and fit themselves to perform specific difficult manual tasks."[5]

— Then President of Princeton University, Woodrow Wilson, in his address to the New York City High School Teachers Association, January 9, 1909

High on the power bestowed upon them by the enormous fortunes made during the industrial revolution, America's industrial titans sought to create an education system that would complement their economic and political interests.

The purpose of this education system would be the same purpose of nearly every government-funded education system anywhere in the world—to advance the interests of those who control the government. More specifically, the aim was to create obedient, docile, and unthinking employees who would be conditioned for life in the factory, where their freedom was stripped and their autonomy nonexistent.

Ironically, the education system was meant to ensure that the citizenry was never truly educated and that they lived their entire lives believing the illusion of their rulers. The propaganda disseminated by the elites is why millions of people are living in a cave of illusions.

It's hard to think there's anything malevolent about the institution of public school since we associate school with education and education with progress. If we remember our own days in elementary school, middle school, or high school, many of us may remember the dull assignments and the relentless boredom caused by learning things with no apparent real-world application. We may also remember the rare teacher who really did have

9

a positive impact on our life. By and large, many who attended public school had a mixed experience, something that wasn't particularly enjoyable but mandated by society to progress in life.

Without knowledge of history and human nature, it's difficult to intuit that something monstrous is going on in classrooms across America, yet the greatest crime is being committed with our consent and complicity. The act of indoctrinating children and drilling blind obedience to authority violates the founding principles of our nation. What exactly is wrong with the public school system? First, it's not "public" in the sense that we have any say in important matters like what children will learn, how they will be taught, or who will teach them.

At the macro level, the public has no say in what children learn; instead, an undemocratic group controls: 1) incentives teachers are subjected to, 2) the curriculum children will learn, and 3) the incentives students are given to promote obedience and punish critical thinking. When you control the incentives teachers and students have and you control the K-12 curriculum, you have the power to modify behavior, mold character, and dull the minds of millions of people. If you wanted to maintain control over a democratic nation of millions of people, what would be the best education system? The late comedic legend George Carlin said it best,

> "Governments don't want a population capable of critical thinking, they want obedient workers, people just smart enough to run the machines and just dumb enough to passively accept their situation."

Obedience and conformity are absolutely necessary if a small group intend on dominating a nation of democratic traditions. The genesis of public school is illuminating in understanding it's founding and present purpose.

Alexander James Inglis, a highly influential educator and prominent Harvard professor, tells us what the real purpose of public education is in his book *The Principles of Secondary Education,* published in 1918.

Inglis took Taylorism, the scientific management of employees, and applied this wartime efficiency to schools. He set out six objectives that public schools were to carry out.[6]

1. *The adjustive or adaptive function*
   Inglis details the importance of inculcating children with "fixed habits of reaction," but to what is ambiguous. To create a fixed habit of reaction, one must destroy critical thinking. Additionally, to control the reactions of children, they must be trained in conformity. An example of a fixed habit of reaction would be a student internalizing that rewards in school are based not on original thought or curiosity but on parroting the teacher's thoughts. Children learn quickly that their thoughts and interests are meaningless. This all has a distinct purpose in the desired character development that the elite seek to ingrain in the masses.
2. *The integrating function*
   "One of the imperative demands made by society on the secondary school is...the development of...unity of thought, habits, ideals, and standards..." Schools are

to make children as standardized as possible so that their conformity makes them predictable. If school is in the best interest of students, why do they pressure students into destroying their uniqueness and making them all alike? Society does not inherently demand conformity of thought, habit, and ideals, but control by a powerful minority over an overwhelming majority does require predictable malleability in the majority. Is that conducive to healthy human development or the maximization of each child's potential? Would you prefer your child to be engineered to be a sheep or an autonomous and creative individual who self-directs their life?

3. *The diagnostic and directive function*
Each child will be continuously graded and tested on standardized exams, and their proper social role will depend on their performance. The exams will test nothing but obedience, which is the chief objective of public school. Obedience is a necessary lubricant to allow oligarchs to rule an ostensible republic. What happens to an intelligent student who doesn't want to waste time on the mindless assignments demanded by their teachers? If they receive below-average grades, is that representative of their intellectual ability or their inability to be obedient? Again, should obedience be an ideal in our nation? I'm not suggesting anarchy and lawlessness but the right each person has not to be brainwashed or indoctrinated.

4. *The differentiating function*
   Once a child is diagnosed with their proper social role, they will be educated insofar as it is necessary for that specific role but no further. A student who is unwilling to spend time studying for exams that are pointless will not be able to earn a piece of paper that tells employers he is sufficiently obedient for the life of an employee. One thing I learned from being an honor roll public school student and college graduate is that the most important thing you can learn is to teach yourself. You may not know all the answers, but if you know the right questions to ask, you can find the answer. If you constantly depend on formal teaching to learn, you'll accomplish nothing great. The best teachers help their students help themselves.

5. *The selective function*
   Social Darwinism through standardized testing. The dumb should be publicly humiliated, and their opportunities for procreation diminished. Your college alma mater greatly affects your social status in society. If you graduate from Harvard, it's assumed you're highly intelligent, but if you're a high school dropout, society considers you a failure. Ironically, many of America's greatest citizens did not have college degrees, and many of America's infamous criminals come from Ivy League universities. In short, grades and scholastic accomplishment mean nothing within a system whose chief purpose is the preservation of the elite's power.

6. *The propaedeutic function*
   Certain students are chosen for further education based on their ability to parrot the commands of their schoolmasters. From this group, future leaders are selected.

Ellwood Cubberley was a contemporary of Dr. Inglis and served as the Dean of the Stanford Graduate School of Education, as well as the chief of elementary school texts at Houghton Mifflin publishing house. In 1916, Cubberley published *Public School Administration* and echoed Inglis' sentiments on the purpose of schooling:

> "Our schools are, in a sense, factories, in which the raw products (children) are to be shaped and fashioned into products to meet the various demands of life. The specifications for manufacturing come from the demands of twentieth-century civilization, and it is the business of the school to build its pupils according to the specifications laid down."[7]

Public school appeared to be a gift to the American people, but its purpose was to subvert an enemy. The enemy public schools sought to destroy were freethinkers and those with high-minded ideals, such as truth, freedom, and justice. To be even more refined, the enemy were people who couldn't be controlled by the tools used by social engineers.

Americans gave unenlightened men access to the minds of their children. With this unprecedented access, these men imposed their will on the young. They wanted to preserve their power by making the population easy to control. Public school fulfilled this purpose by deliberately destroying freethinking and curiosity in children.

The history of why and how public education came to be in the United States is of supreme relevance.

In the mid-nineteenth century, Massachusetts was the first state to adopt compulsory public schooling. Horace Mann led the reform movement, citing his admiration for the Prussian education system first set up in 1819. After Napoleon defeated the Prussians during the Napoleonic Wars, they sought to create a system of education that would instill its citizenry with unquestioning obedience to authority and prevent any future military defeats.

Past is prologue. Where did the Prussian education system lead Germany? Prussian-style education gave birth to a German epoch that would lead Germans to support three aggressive wars—the Franco-German War of 1870, World War I, and, of course, World War II. Prussian education destroyed the critical thinking abilities of the German people and led them to democratically elect the Nazis and force German President Paul Von Hindenburg to appoint Hitler chancellor in 1933. When a population loses the ability to think, question, and value the truth, dictators soon follow.

The American system of public education championed by Horace Mann followed the same ideal of obedience to authority. Assuming Mann's intentions were virtuous, he made a critical miscalculation. He acknowledged that the Prussian education system served the nation's elite, not the children, but he naively thought that public education in America could serve benevolent republican ends.

In his Seventh Annual Report to the Massachusetts Board of Education in 1843, Mann said:

"If Prussia can pervert the benign influence of education to the support of arbitrary power, we surely can employ them for the support of and perpetuation of republican institutions. A national spirit of liberty can be cultivated more easily than a national spirit of bondage; and, if it may be made one of the great prerogatives of education to perform the unnatural and unholy work of making slaves, then surely it must be one of the noblest instrumentalities for rearing a nation of freemen. If a moral power over the understandings and affections of the people may be turned to evil, may it not also be employed for good?"[8]

Horace Mann forgot about one thing: the ability of human beings to be corrupted and the ability for institutions to be hijacked to serve the powerful. Mann's push for public education created a powerful institution that allowed the government, and therefore anyone who controlled the government, to have twelve years to mold the minds of the nation's young with unrestricted access.

The public debate that preceded the establishment of compulsory schooling in Massachusetts reveals the alarmingly accurate foresight that critics had in the mid-nineteenth century. In 1839, Orestes Brownson, a New England intellectual and activist, criticized the compulsory schooling proposals, remarking in an essay entitled *In Opposition to Centralization* (1839):

"The truth is, we have, in the establishment of this board of education, undertaken to imitate despotic Prussia, without considering the immense distance between the two countries...in Prussia the whole business of education is lodged in the hands of government. The government establishes the schools in which it prepares the teachers; it determines both the methods of teaching and the matters taught. It commissions all teachers and suffers no one to engage in teaching without authority from itself. Who sees not then that all the teachers will be the pliant tools of the government and that the whole tendency of the education given will be to make the Prussians obedient subjects of Frederic the king? Who sees not that education in Prussia is supported merely as the most efficient arm of the police and fostered merely for the purpose of keeping out revolutionary or, what is the same thing liberal ideas? A government system of education in Prussia is not inconsistent with the theory of Prussian society, for there all wisdom is supposed to be lodged in the government, but the thing is wholly inadmissible here not because government may be in the hands of Whigs or Democrats, but because, according to our theory the people are wiser than the government. Here the people do not look to the government for light, for instruction, but the government looks to the people. The people give law to the government. To entrust government with the power of determining education which our children shall receive is entrusting our servant with the power to be our master...In a

> free government, there can be no teaching by authority, and all attempts to teach by authority are so many blows struck at its freedom...Government is not in this country, and cannot be, the educator of the people. In education, as in religion, we must rely mainly on the voluntary system."[9]

Would there have been an American Revolution if the Founding Fathers were brainwashed by a compulsory schooling system ordained by King George III? Those in power think differently than you do. Their frame of reference is alien to you because you do not share their concerns, fears, and ambitions. The power structure fears revolution. They are concerned they will one day lose their ability to manipulate and, unleashed, the citizenry would throw them from their high places. They fear that their main tool of control, namely illusions, will be uncovered and the prison they have so thoughtfully invested in will be destroyed.

Public school is a strategic maneuver to brainwash the young who will grow into adulthood holding beliefs, worldviews, and pervasive ignorance that allows the elite to rule unimpeded by democratic demands. Critics of public education saw what the real purpose was and the deleterious consequences it would have on a free society. The consequences are devasting. By brainwashing children, it creates intellectual gaps that propaganda can exploit and ensures people are malleable to manipulation. This allows those in power to manufacture consent for wars of aggression, turn intelligence agencies on the American people, use terrorism to achieve political ends, and manipulate people to be consumer robots. The benefits of public education to the elite are priceless, while the damage done to the minds of millions is immeasurable. The elite declared war on Americans and sought to conquer them in the same way an invading army conquers a native population.

Brownson was not the only critic of government-controlled education. Writing in his treatise, *On Liberty*, English philosopher John Stuart Mill poignantly remarked:

> "A general state education is a mere contrivance for molding people to be exactly like one another; and as the mold in which it casts them is that which pleases the predominant power in the government, whether this be a monarch, a priesthood or an aristocracy, or the majority of the existing generation, in proportion as it is efficient and successful, it establishes a despotism over the mind, leading by natural tendency to one over the body."[10]

H.L. Mencken, the famous American social critic of the early twentieth century, vehemently lampooned public education for the same reasons used by Orestes Brownson and John Stuart Mill.

Mencken remarked:

> "The erroneous assumption is to the effect that the aim of public education is to fill the young of the species with knowledge and awaken their intelligence, and so make them fit to discharge the duties of citizenship in

Peter Magistrale

an enlightened and independent manner. Nothing could be further from the truth. The aim of public education is not to spread enlightenment at all; it is simply to reduce as many individuals as possible to the same safe level, to breed and train a standardized citizenry, to put down dissent and originality. That is its aim in the United States, whatever the pretensions of politicians ...and that is its aim everywhere else...Their purpose, in brief, is to make docile and patriotic citizens, to pile up majorities, to make John Doe and Richard Doe as nearly alike, in their everyday reactions and ways of thinking, as possible."[11]

"If their fundamental aim is to provide the country with an enlightened electorate, they have failed completely and miserably, for the electorate is no more enlightened today than it was before they were ever set up. On the contrary, there is plausible reason for believing that it has gone backward in intelligence, for it handles its business, not with increasing prudence, but with increasing imbecility. The American people of a hundred years ago, when public schools were still few and meagre, might have been described plausibly as notably political-minded; they were ardently interested in public affairs, and intervened in them, on the whole, with quick understanding and sound judgment. But today they are so lethargic that it takes a calamity to arouse them at all, and so stupid that it becomes more nearly impossible every year for intelligent and self-respecting men to aspire to public office among them."[12]

The first crime committed against all American children is to brainwash them with the power the state has over schooling. Of course, the state is nothing but an agent of the wealthy and powerful. From this crime, all crimes follow in consequential succession. The child's mind is prepared for the lies, deceptions, and illusions they will be bombarded with later in life. The public school brainwashing program creates a fertile ground for the corrupt rulers of society. Can you imagine how much corporate profits would decline if people were taught the deceptions of propaganda and marketing and thus did not practice mindless consumerism? Can you imagine how difficult it would be to control 320 million people if they were trained in critical thinking, history, and leadership? Can you imagine how hard it would be to persuade people to engage in preemptive aggressive war if they were not blindly loyal to authority figures who cunningly wrap themselves in the American flag?

We must understand the motives of the people who rule America. They know their power is illegitimate within the founding principles of our nation. They feel compelled to deploy social controls because left to their own volition the elite know the American people would imprison them or worse. The elite understand history and human nature. Since we were purposely robbed of acquiring this knowledge as part of our indoctrination, let us begin with the obvious.

A society where too many people are freethinkers is a potentially unstable society. If assumptions underlying society are constantly questioned, the elite live in a perpetually perilous position. It's difficult to convince people they are free, let them vote, but in reality, control every important aspect of their lives.

This is intellectual gymnastics that only a well-propagandized mind can passively accept. The elite mold the minds of children, and with that influence, they avoid revolution.

For those who believe that the purpose of public school has miraculously become benevolent in the recent past, there is no evidence it has. The public school of 2020 is no different in fundamental purpose from the public school of 1920, and that's with trillions more of funding.

Bill Gates spent millions to mold a national K-12 curriculum, and the Obama Administration centralized it by attaching federal funding only if states adopted Common Core. Is Bill Gates an elected official? Is he accountable to the public? Did the public really have any influence or choice in what their children would learn or how they would learn? No on all accounts.

Common Core forces teachers to teach to the test and, no different from public school a hundred years ago, the real thing being tested is obedience to stupid and boring tasks. A perfect example is elementary Common Core Math. Here are a few examples of the imbecility of the curriculum.

> Question: Tell me how to make 10 when adding 8 + 5.
> Student's Answer: You cannot make 10 with 8 + 5.
> Teacher's Response: Yes, you can. Take 2 from 5 and add it to 8. 8+2 = 10.

Here's another question with a ridiculous answer.

> Question: Carole read 28 pages of a book on Monday and read a total 103 pages by Tuesday. Is 75 pages a

reasonable answer for how many more pages Carole read on Tuesday than on Monday?

Student's Answer: Yes, 75 pages is a reasonable answer because 103 - 28 = 75.

Teacher's Response: Wrong answer. Correct answer is to estimate 100 - 30 = 70.

Public school today is a disgrace due to the continued top-down structure and the continued efforts by elites to ensure conformity and obedience are ingrained in the nation's children, ensuring they will be good wage slaves, mindless consumers, and ignorant voters in later life.

When the purpose and cost of public education is understood, it becomes infuriating. New York is a perfect example of a state that is robbing taxpayers to fund the indoctrination center known as public school.

In 2017, New York State spent more than $23,000 to educate each student who attended public school.[13] By 2021, this figure will be north of $25,000 per pupil. If we assume, for simplicity purposes, that the annual cost per pupil remains the same, New Yorkers will pay approximately $325,000 to educate each child who enters kindergarten in 2021 and graduates thirteen years later in 2034. The poetic irony is striking. New Yorkers pay $325,000 to have their children brainwashed in conformity and blind obedience.

Let's say each family received $25,000 per school-age child per year to educate their children as they saw best. Further, let's say a hypothetical family has triplets, spends $10,000 each year to educate each child, invests the remaining $45,000 ([$25,000

- $10,000] *3 children) in the S&P 500 index fund, and earns 7% per year for thirteen years. The investment would grow to about $900,000 by the time the three children reach eighteen years old. Furthermore, let's assume each child goes to a state school or gets a decent academic scholarship and winds up paying $60,000 for four years of college. For simplicity purposes, let's assume this investment is worth $700,000 at the end of the four years and it's split into three equal parts and given to each child to help fund their future retirement.

Each child would have about $233,000 at twenty-two years old. If this amount were invested in a plain vanilla total U.S. stock market index fund and yielded 7% annualized returns after inflation until the children reach retirement age of sixty-five, the $233,000 would grow to approximately $4.3 million.

At thirty-five years old, each adult would have about $560,000, and at forty-seven years old, each adult would have about $1.26 million in these investment accounts. The New York State government will waste millions in taxpayer funds to educate each child in nothing but standardization and obedience. If someone steals money from you today, your loss is not the absolute amount lost today but the loss in decades of compounded returns

The educational reformer John Dewey wrote in his "Pedagogic Creed Statement of 1897,"

> "Every teacher should realize he is a social servant set apart for the maintenance of the proper social order and the securing of the right social growth. In this way the

teacher is always the prophet of the true God and the usherer in of the true kingdom of heaven."[14]

Who determines the proper social order? Of course, the powerful do, and what social order do they seek to create? A stable society where they are free to impose their will on the masses. How do the elite guarantee the masses swallow their propaganda? Simply by preemptively dumbing them down from ages five to seventeen and making obedience an ideal.

The self-taught British sociologist Benjamin Kidd wrote *In The Science of Power*, "The main cause of those deep diving differences which separate peoples and nationalities and classes from each other and which prevent or stultify collective effort in all its most powerful forms...could all be swept away if civilization put before itself the will to impose on the young the ideal of subordination to the common aims of organized humanity...So to impose it has become the chief end of education in the future...Give us the young and we will create a new mind and new earth in a single generation."[15]

Again, who determines the common aims of organized humanity? The powerful do. Since the elite control society, Kidd suggested the young be indoctrinated to accept the ideal of obedience. Obedience makes management of large populations much more efficient and less troublesome. It allows for the circumvention of conventional avenues of societal change and expedites the brainwashing process.

With the support of funding from the Department of Education, Health, and Welfare, the University of Michigan published the feasibility study of the Behavioral Science Teacher Education Project in 1969.[16]

After 247 pages of mind-numbing writing, the authors evaluate how future social changes could affect public education and educators. The authors posited by foreseeing future developments that education would change with the times to remain relevant. Here are three predictions made by the University of Michigan in 1969:

Futurism as a Social Tool and Decision-Making by an Elite

"... Long-range planning and implementation of plans will be made by a technological-scientific elite. Political democracy, in the American ideological sense, will be limited to broad social policy; even there, issues, alternatives, and means will be so complex that the elite will be influential to a degree which will arouse the fear and animosity of others. This will strain the democratic fabric to a ripping point."

A Controlling Elite

"The Protestant Ethic will atrophy as more and more enjoy varied leisure and guaranteed sustenance. Work as the means and end of living will diminish in importance except for a few with exceptional motivation, drive, or aspiration. No major source of a sense of worth and dignity will replace the Protestant Ethic. Most people will tend to be hedonistic, and a dominant elite will provide 'bread and circuses' to keep social dissension and disruption to a minimum. A small elite will carry society's burdens. The resulting impersonal manipulation of most people's lifestyles will be softened by provisions for pleasure seeking and guaranteed physical necessities. Participatory democracy in the American-ideal mold will mainly disappear. The worth and dignity of individuals will be endangered on every hand. Only exceptional individuals will be able to maintain a sense of worth and dignity."

Here's what they said in a more refined form: "Long range planning...will be done by a technological-scientific elite... who will provide bread and circuses to keep social dissension and disruption to a minimum...The resulting impersonal manipulation of most people's life styles will be softened by provisions for pleasure seeking and guaranteed physical necessities. Participatory democracy in the American-ideal mold will mainly disappear. The worth and dignity of individuals will be endangered on every hand. Only exceptional individuals will be able to maintain a sense of worth and dignity."

That was a prediction in 1969. Today, that is largely a reality. The evidence is sufficient beyond doubt that the nation's economic and political elite have contempt for democracy, individual liberty, and the founding ideals of our nation.

From 1900 to 1920, Andrew Carnegie and David Rockefeller provided more funding for public schools than the federal government.[17] Money was invented to buy things. What did they buy, and what was the educational philosophy of these financiers? Did they ascribe to the Enlightenment ideal of education—that of kindling a flame—or the command and control view that education was similar to filling an empty cup?

The first mission statement of David Rockefeller's General Education Board outlined in Occasional Letter Number One makes it very clear:

> "In our dream, we have limitless resources and the people yield themselves with perfect docility to our molding hand. The present educational conventions fade from their minds; and, unhampered by tradition, we work our own good will upon a grateful and responsive rural folk. We shall not try to make these people or any of their children into philosophers or men of learning, or men of science. We have not to raise up from among them authors, editors, poets or men of letters. We shall not search for embryo great artists, painters, musicians nor lawyers, doctors, preachers, politicians, statesmen, of whom we have an ample supply...The task we set before ourselves is very simple as well as a very beautiful one, to train these people as we find them to a perfectly ideal life just where they are...So we will organize our children into a little community and teach them to do in a perfect way the things their fathers and mothers are doing in an imperfect way, in the homes, in the shops and on the farm."[18]

Note that a philosopher is someone who loves truth and wisdom, and they had no use for such people.

What is the significance of all this? Public school was built to carry out the will of wealthy business interests. Think about what an ideal employee is to a corporation.

He is obedient; he follows orders and conforms to the demands of management. He is predictable using stick and carrot methods. He is a resource no different from copper or wheat to be used to maximize profit, and most egregious, he is to never dwell on the fact that he is not free.

Of course, they had no use for philosophers or anyone who couldn't be scientifically managed. Such people are unpredictable and can't be kept in servitude for long. Public school teaches children that the only way to succeed is to be blindly obedient to their teachers, to accept that truth comes from authority, and to conform at every turn to established norms, all of which produces childlike adults and perfect employees for corporations that view people as expendable resources. The great figures of history are freethinkers who act autonomously and pursue the realization of their potential. This crime of purposely brainwashing children makes the next crime of the wealthy possible.

Siphoning the Nation's Wealth

When you have a nation of people whose minds are destroyed by thirteen years of behavior modification, it's much easier to commit high crimes without anyone holding you accountable. Truth comes from power. Never question people who know more than you do. Focus on yourself. These are the great lessons learned in public school. Of course, these lessons are applied in real life with disastrous consequences.

The Department of Defense (DoD) is ground zero for high crimes committed by our government. Of all the crimes committed within the DoD, none is more palpable than the DoD's wholesale robbery of our nation's wealth. How much does the federal government steal from us?

In 2001 alone, the DoD could not account for $2.4 trillion in transactions.[19] In 1990, a federal law was passed mandating that all federal agencies be subject to annual audits. The DoD was audited for the first time twenty-eight years later in 2018, and, unsurprisingly, it failed the audit.[20] This lack of accountability is not isolated to the DoD. This is symptomatic of the entire federal government. Graft, corruption, waste, and abuse are the norm. Corporate America routinely loses 5% of revenues to fraud even with internal controls mandated by Sarbanes-Oxley.[21] Ironically, the federal government does not have to adhere to the internal controls it mandates public companies follow. With this understood, it's reasonable to conclude that the DoD loses up to 20% of taxpayer money to fraud, abuse, waste, and other types of corruption, while other agencies and programs lose up to 15%.

In the first twenty years of the twenty-first century, America will spend more than $10 trillion on defense. At a 15%–25% waste rate, we are taking about $1.5–$2.5 trillion of taxes Americans paid for no good reason. It all seems distant and impersonal, but let's get personal. The money you work so hard to earn goes to a government that will waste no less than 15% of it. Each year the income taxes you pay in January and February are completely wasted. Let's say you and your spouse have a combined average income of $150,000 over your 40-year working career. You each graduate from college making $50,000 per year, midway through you both make $75,000, and you retire at sixty-five making $100,000 each. The federal government stole approximately $200,000 from you, but if you had invested that money each year instead of enriching a few wealthy corporations and earned 8% per year over those forty years, the government would have stolen $1 million from you and your family. That wealth went to such companies as Boeing, Lockheed Martin, and Halliburton. Without war and enemies, these companies don't make money, so they are sure to invent new enemies and steal as much as they can from everyday Americans. This wealth extraction has devastated the lives of millions of honest, hardworking Americans, and ending this robbery would have exceptional effects on our posterity. How many Americans are struggling to meet ends meet, going into bankruptcy to pay medical bills, and saddled by debt? With the amount of financial corruption and waste, it's a miracle anything works, but ending this persistent crime and reallocating resources in a more thoughtful manner could yield exceptional benefits to the American people.

WAR AND TERRORISM

Aggressive war reinforces the prevailing power structure. It's an age-old strategy used by ancient empires, current-day dictators, and ostensible democracies. The strategy is simple: manipulate the population into a primitive state of mind so that fear, vengeance, and blind patriotism overrule reason, common sense, and justice. This emotional and irrational state strengthens the illusions that keep the population imprisoned, manufactures an external enemy so the people forget who their real enemies are, and stimulates the economy for corporations owned by the wealthy. After World War II, the decision to go to war in America has been largely decided by the elite. Once they determine war is the agenda, consent is manufactured through propaganda. The elite declare war because it rationally serves their interests. They then manipulate the middle class and poor to fight the wars they declare. The brainwashing works because the majority can't think well enough to identify lies and deceptions.

This perennial crime wasted no time to strike in the opening years of the twenty-first century.

A nation of uncritical citizens makes happy leaders. When George W. Bush wanted to declare war on Iraq but had no real evidence or reason to justify a war, he remembered that evidence and reason are not necessary for effective public persuasion. With the support of the ministry of propaganda, otherwise known as the mainstream media, you can bend public consent to your will. Their will was aggressive war to achieve geopolitical objectives as well as enrich their cronies.

The war in Iraq was a monumental failure not only for America as a whole but also for our values. Not only did we elect one of the most incompetent presidents in our history, but we also did it twice. We succumbed to fear, we didn't question a thing, and we went along for the ignorant ride. As a result of this lack of critical thinking, we gave an irresponsible person eight years of unaccountability and free rein to violate the good name Americans worked hard to earn all across the globe.

Instead of educating ourselves on topics that matter, such as justification to start a preemptive war, we instead subjugate our minds to less complicated topics, such as football, reality

TV, *American Idol*, *The X Factor*, *Dancing With the Stars*, and the list goes on. If someone lies to you, do you blindly trust them the next time they tell you something important? Most people wouldn't when it comes to their personal relationships, but we inexplicably follow authority figures with religious devotion.

If you aren't aware of the blatant lies and lack of character on the part of George W. Bush to manipulate the American people into accepting the Iraq War, prepare for a devastating rebuke of all we were told. There is substantial evidence that proves George W. Bush lied about Saddam Hussein's threat to America and used those lies as a pretext for an illegal war that killed thousands of American soldiers and hundreds of thousands of Iraqis, all the while achieving nothing. This war, justified by lies, will cost the United States more than $5 trillion in the first half of the twenty-first century.[22] In every regard, it was a grotesque dismemberment of our republic.

Let's start with what a lie is because that is why thousands of people have died. The dictionary definition is "a false statement made with deliberate intent to deceive." The facts to follow will prove President Bush was made privy of certain information and then contradicted this information without basis in addresses to the public and Congress.

The first significant part of President Bush's campaign to convince the nation that Iraq needed to be invaded was that Saddam Hussein was an imminent threat to the security of the U.S. Before we examine the lies, let's first consider two examples in which Bush and his administration spoke in this manner. First, Secretary of Defense Donald Rumsfeld on September

33

18, 2002, addressed the Armed Forces Committee and bluntly stated:

> "Some have argued that the nuclear threat from Iraq is not imminent, that Saddam is at least 5–7 years away from having nuclear weapons. I would not be so certain. And we should be just as concerned about the immediate threat from biological weapons. Iraq has these weapons."[23]

On October 7, 2002, President Bush spoke at the Museum Center in Cincinnati where he said:

> "Some ask how urgent this danger is to America and the world. The danger is already significant, and it only grows worse with time...America must not ignore the threat gathering against us. Facing clear evidence of peril, we cannot wait for the final proof—the smoking gun—that could come in the form of a mushroom cloud."[24]

These are not two cherry-picked comments; they are an accurate sample of Bush and his administration's rhetoric leading Americans and Congress to think that the threat was imminent and that a preemptive attack was justified.

As the above quote states, Bush gave a speech on October 7 that included a comment that gave the audience the impression that the threat was imminent. Two questions people should be asking themselves: (1) what information was our president basing these strong assertions on, and (2) who was the source of this evidence?

Six days before his Cincinnati speech, the CIA garnished the president with the National Intelligence Estimate (NIE), a report summarizing the opinions of sixteen U.S. intelligence agencies. In the 2002 NIE, it said, among other things, that:

> "Baghdad, for now, appears to be drawing the line short of conducting terrorist attacks with conventional or CBW (chemical or biological weapons) against the United States, fearing that exposure of Iraqi involvement would provide Washington a stronger case for making war. Iraq probably would attempt a clandestine attack if Baghdad feared an attack that threatened the survival of the regime were imminent or unavoidable."[25]

In other words, the consensus of the U.S. intelligence community was that Iraq was not an imminent threat to the security of America, yet six days later Bush was on national television telling the American people that Iraq presented a significant danger to the security of the U.S., and there was clear evidence of peril. The words he used connoted imminent danger as if Iraqi warships were off the coast of Cape Cod aiming their guns at the homeland.

In reality, Bush lied, and we know he lied because the 2002 NIE given to Bush six days before the speech didn't believe there was an imminent threat posed by Iraq. Which begs the question, why in the world was he making such outlandish comments that contradicted sixteen intelligence agencies? Further evidence that Bush lied about Iraq's imminent threat at his Cincinnati speech was that his own CIA director and close advisor wrote a letter to Senator Bob Graham on October 7, 2002 (day of Bush's speech), echoing the NIE report. George Tenet wrote, "Baghdad, for now, appears to be drawing a line short of conducting terrorist attacks with conventional or CBW (chemical or biological weapons) against the United States."[26]

Vincent Bugliosi, a retired Los Angeles County prosecutor best known for prosecuting serial killer Charles Manson and for his near-perfect conviction rate of 104–105 cases, wrote in his 2008 *New York Times* best-seller, *The Prosecution of George W. Bush For Murder*, referring to the letter from Tenet to Graham, "...a source at the CIA headquarters in Langley, Virginia, told me (in a telephone conversation on March 10, 2003) that the date of the letter was October 7, 2002, and the physical letter itself was couriered to Graham that same day, October 7, before Bush's speech that night. Senator Graham's press office told me that the message was also faxed to Graham's office at 4:27 p.m. on October 7."[27]

The bottom line is that Tenet briefed Bush on the morning of October 7 and told him that Iraq didn't pose an imminent threat to the U.S., yet Bush with this knowledge decided to use language that wasn't consistent with that of his own CIA director. It's clear as day that President Bush contradicted the opinions of sixteen intelligence agencies, including his own CIA director, when he made a speech in Cincinnati that used language consistent with Iraq being an imminent threat, an absolute lie that began to turn the nation in favor of the war.

On July 23, 2002, British foreign policy aide Matthew Rycroft wrote a memo of a meeting between British Prime Minister, Tony Blair and his advisors on Iraq. According to the memo, Sir Richard Dearlove, Britain's Secret Intelligence chief (Head of MI6), told Blair that from his discussions in Washington with Bush administration officials it was clear that, "Bush wanted to remove Saddam, through military action, justified by the conjunction of terrorism and WMD. But the intelligence and facts were being fixed around the policy."[28]

This is direct documented evidence from high in Britain's government that proves, without a doubt, that Bush and his administration "fixed" or lied, manipulating information to achieve predetermined goals. Why would the Bush administration need to fix intelligence and facts if they weren't lying?

We have heard how Bush lied to the American people regarding Saddam's threat to the U.S. and how a memo from a British official said the Bush administration was fixing facts and intelligence around the policy. Another crystal-clear example of deceit on the part of the Bush administration to scare the American people into submission was their claim that Iraq was seeking uranium from Niger. This statement implied that if Saddam could acquire uranium, he would be very close to building a nuclear bomb and potentially use it on America. Against the advice of numerous intelligence agencies, President Bush introduced this threat to the American people at his State of the Union address on January 28, 2003, stating that the "British Government has learned that Saddam Hussein recently sought significant quantities of uranium from Africa."

The British report was based on a document that several investigations concluded was forged, and that the sale never happened. Subsequently, President Bush was made aware of these investigations and still used the disproved and discredited report to instill fear in the American people; hence another lie smacked the American conscience. One of the two well-known investigations into the matter was conducted in February 2002 by former ambassador to Iraq, Joseph Wilson. Summoned by Vice President Cheney, Wilson conducted an 8-day investigation and reported back to the CIA that the occurrence of the transaction in question most likely didn't occur. In a July 6, 2003, op-ed article in the *New York Times* "What I Didn't Find in Africa," Wilson referring to the likelihood of the sale said, "It did not take long to conclude that it was highly doubtful that any such transaction had ever taken place."[29]

Corroborating Wilson's conclusions were France's National Spy Service. In a December 11, 2005, article published in the *Los Angeles Times* "French Told CIA of Bogus Intelligence," former counterintelligence chief of France's national spy service, Alain Chouet, told the paper that he had summoned multiple investigations stemming from the British report for the period 2001–2002, and every investigation concluded there was no evidence that Saddam Hussein sought to or purchased uranium from Niger.[30]

Furthermore, Chouet shared his findings with the CIA well in advance of President Bush's 2003 State of the Union address and was utterly stunned when he heard President Bush say that Iraq was seeking uranium from Africa. French experts viewed

We The People Are The Problem

Bush's Iraq-Uranium-Africa claim as, "...totally crazy because, in our view, there was no backup for this."

Once again, on what basis did our president make such a claim? If French intelligence had concluded that Saddam wasn't seeking uranium and our own Joseph Wilson came to the same conclusion, then what did the Bush administration know that they didn't? Even though several investigations concluded that Saddam didn't seek uranium from Niger, there is more evidence that Bush lied at his 2003 State of the Union address. Investigative journalist Craig Unger investigated the Niger claims for his 2006 piece in *Vanity Fair*. For thoroughness, he interviewed many CIA and DIA (Defense Intelligence Agency) officials who worked for these agencies leading up to the 2003 State of the Union address. Unger found fourteen examples preceding the 2003 State of the Union address in which members of the CIA and DIA questioned the validity of the Niger documents, "...only to be rebuffed by Bush administration officials who wanted to use them."[31]

Overall, President Bush was told by the 2002 NIE and George Tenet himself that Iraq wasn't an imminent threat, was told by Joseph Wilson and French intelligence that there was no evidence to support the claim that Saddam was seeking uranium from Niger, and used a PR scheme based on lies to manipulate Congress and the American people into accepting an Iraqi invasion.

Any rational person would have to conclude that the Harvard Business School graduate George W. Bush had the mental capacity to process information and lied at his 2003 State of the Union address and his Cincinnati speech. This

39

deception and the collective lies that Bush and his administration told America led to the unnecessary deaths of people who had dreams, people who had families, and people who will never see the light of day again. More than five hundred thousand Iraqis, and more than seven thousand of our best and most courageous soldiers should be alive today.

President Bush and many in the Bush administration are war criminals empowered by American ignorance and blind patriotism. It is that persistent public ignorance that time and time again enables high crimes.

In the fall of 2004, the *New York Times* published an article written by Ron Suskind. His interaction with a senior Bush advisor is very telling in understanding the criminal psychology of those whose actions led to needless deaths, carnage, and trillions in waste.

> "In the summer of 2002, after I had written an article in *Esquire* that the White House didn't like about Bush's former communications director, Karen Hughes, I had a meeting with a senior adviser to Bush. He expressed the White House's displeasure, and then he told me something that at the time I didn't fully comprehend—but which I now believe gets to the very heart of the Bush presidency.
>
> The aide said that guys like me were, 'in what we call the reality-based community,' which he defined as people who 'believe that solutions emerge from your judicious study of discernible reality.' I nodded and murmured

something about enlightenment principles and empiricism. He cut me off. 'That's not the way the world really works anymore,' he continued. 'We're an empire now, and when we act, we create our own reality. And while you're studying that reality—judiciously, as you will—we'll act again, creating other new realities, which you can study too, and that's how things will sort out. We're history's actors...and you, all of you, will be left to just study what we do.'"[32]

PROPAGANDA

Whether the wealthy are selling cigarettes, war, or a presidential candidate, propaganda is their weapon of choice. The body cannot tolerate cancer indefinitely, and a society cannot be free with propaganda in its midst. There is a psychological war going on in which the American psyche is the battlefield, and propaganda is the weapon. Propaganda is the use of deceptive and manipulative communication techniques that utilize extensive psychological knowledge to brainwash an individual. It acts like a Trojan horse on the mind. It is so effective because it bypasses the rational aspect of the human psyche and exploits the irrational aspect, turning people into robots who will obey the commands of their unseen masters.

It's stunning to reflect on how Adolf Hitler convinced the German people to hate Jews, love lies, and embrace the Nazi ideology. Many people are unaware that among the many weapons Hitler deployed, none was more important than the creation of the Ministry of Propaganda. To understand

41

Hitler's worldview and opinion of the ordinary person, consider this excerpt from Hitler's autobiography, *Mein Kampf*.

> "The broad masses of the people are not made up of diplomats or professors of public jurisprudence nor simply of persons who can form reasoned judgment in given cases, but a vacillating crowd of human children who are constantly wavering between one idea and another...The great majority of a nation is so feminine in its character and outlook that its thought and conduct are ruled by sentiment rather than by sober reasoning."[33]

We all know that Hitler employed propaganda, but what most of us do not know is that he was not the first to perfect it. Propaganda was perfected in the early twentieth century right here in the United States. A key figure in the U.S. propaganda machine aimed toward the American people was Edward Bernays. He is considered the founding father of modern day public relations because of his contributions to so many public relations campaigns on behalf of the business community and the U.S. government during World War I. He used psychologically deceptive techniques to "engineer consent."

Consider this quote that exemplifies Edward Bernays' elitist world view.

> "The conscious and intelligent manipulation of the organized habits and opinions of the masses is an important element in democratic society. Those who manipulate

this unseen mechanism of society constitute an invisible government which is the true ruling power of our country...We are governed, our minds are molded, our tastes formed, our ideas suggested, largely by men we have never heard of. This is a logical result of the way in which our democratic society is organized. Vast numbers of human beings must cooperate in this manner if they are to live together as a smoothly functioning society...In almost every act of our daily lives, whether in the sphere of politics or business, in our social conduct or our ethical thinking, we are dominated by the relatively small number of persons...who understand the mental processes and social patterns of the masses. It is they who pull the wires which control the public mind."[34]

Bernays is describing psychological warfare that the ruling class of this country wages against the people to sustain their power and circumvent democracy.

Another man who was instrumental to public relations propaganda was Ivy Lee. In the spring of 1914, Colorado coal workers were striking for dignified working conditions. One of the coal companies the strike opposed was the Colorado Fuel & Iron Company, owned by John D. Rockefeller Jr. On the morning of April 20, 1914, the Colorado National Guard and Colorado Fuel and Iron Company guards opened fire on the makeshift tent colony in Ludlow, Colorado. They unleashed rifle and machine gun fire on strikers and their families. In the end, twenty-one people were massacred, including eleven children who died by asphyxiation.

Rockefeller was crucified in the press for his responsibility in the needless killings. Ivy Lee was hired to counter this negative press. Lee did what all corporate publicists do. He lied to promote his client's interest. He released a pamphlet that blamed the Ludlow deaths on agitators hired by the United Mine Workers of America. The famous muckraker Upton Sinclair nicknamed Ivy Lee "Poison Ivy" for his indecent obfuscation of the truth regarding the Ludlow Massacre. In the end, the strike was broken, no one was held accountable for the killings, and Rockefeller went on to exponentially increase his family's fortune.[35]

What good is democracy if a small group of powerful interests can use propaganda to control public opinion, and, therefore, public policy? If people can't think, democracy is dead. If public school is the process of building a cage around the mind, then propaganda does more than just keep the lights off. It persuades people the shadows are the truth. All of this is a national disgrace that must be dismantled.

Should the wealthy be allowed to dictate what laws are made in our land, what politicians are elected, and what purpose our institutions serve? Should the wealthy be allowed to dumb down your children with a 13-year brainwashing program called public school? Should the wealthy be allowed to lobby for a $600 billion annual defense budget because it enriches their corporations while impoverishing their fellow Americans?

As a democratic society, we must stop the wealthy from dominating lawmaking. Corporations and the wealthy elite have been running our country in earnest for more than a century. Do you like the America they have built? Do you like paying taxes to a corrupt government that will use your money to hand out contracts to their cronies? Do you like that unelected soulless corporate sociopaths have far more influence over healthcare, war and peace, and education than you do?

The wealthy will give you endless choices in areas of triviality, but concerning power, you have none. If the wealthy understood their civic responsibility, they would be tolerable, even admirable, but too many have contempt for democracy, human achievement, and republican ideals.

There's a reason why our society works for the sole benefit of the American aristocracy: an oligarchy has conquered America. This oligarchy of wealthy families and powerful corporations are destroying the American ideals of individual liberty and democratic power.

This is an oligarchy that sees human beings as resources to be consumed, has utter contempt for our potential as human beings, and whose selfish social engineering would make Adolf Hitler jealous.

Wealth does not give one the right to rule. The American, French, and Russian Revolutions clearly show that humanity will not accept rule by the wealthy, rule by aristocracy, or rule by privilege of birth. We are ruled by the rich, which is a disgrace to the millions who died to stop foreign domination of our nation. Instead, we have succumbed to traitors from within—traitors who embody the ethos of Julius Caesar: wealth over duty.

Andrew Carnegie and John D. Rockefeller were the ultimate traitors. To preserve their economic empires and the burgeoning industrial economy, they destroyed hundreds of millions of young American minds by hijacking public school with the intent to create obedient, passive, brainwashed employees who have no knowledge of anything important and no desire to acquire it. This is an unforgivable betrayal of the highest order.

It's against the Constitution for the rich to pursue in private what can only be legitimately pursued in public. The rich, no matter how virtuous and benevolent, have no right to impose their will on the United States. Of course, some good people use their wealth altruistically, but we must protect our republic from the unenlightened wealthy. We know from the 1953 Congressional investigation by the Reece Committee on tax-exempt foundations that there was evidence that numerous foundations created by wealthy Americans were funding ideas and practices contrary to the U.S. Constitution.

Representative Norman Dodd wrote:

> "It seems incredible that the trustees of typically American fortune-created foundations should have permitted them to be used to finance ideas and practices incompatible with the fundamental concepts of our Constitution. Yet there seems evidence that this may have occurred."[36]

FASCISM IN AMERICA

On April 9, 1944, the *New York Times* published "The Dangers of American Fascism," an op-ed written by Vice President Henry Wallace.

"The really dangerous American fascists are not those who are hooked up directly or indirectly with the Axis. The FBI has its finger on those. The dangerous American fascist is the man who wants to do in the United States in an American way what Hitler did in Germany in a Prussian way. The American fascist would prefer not to use violence. His method is to poison the channels of public information. With a fascist, the problem is never how best to present the truth to the public but how best to use the news to deceive the public into giving the fascist and his group more money or more power.

If we define an American fascist as one who in case of conflict puts money and power ahead of human beings, then there are undoubtedly several million fascists in the United States. There are probably several hundred thousand if we narrow the definition to include only those who in their search for money and power are ruthless and deceitful. Most American fascists are enthusiastically supporting the war effort. They are doing this even in those cases where they hope to have profitable connections with German chemical firms after the war ends. They are patriotic in time of war because it is to their interest to be so, but in time of peace they follow power and the dollar wherever they may lead."[37]

The Nazis lost World War II, but their methods of mass manipulation would be repurposed in the postwar years in the U.S. Why? Simply because they worked. Fascism looks for the most efficient way to gain power and achieve political ends. Many

47

Americans are unaware of how Hitler justified his invasion of Poland. We would be well suited to understand how the Nazis planned and executed Operation Himmler. In the months leading up to August 1939, Hitler's chief political end was aggressive war against Poland on Germany's eastern border, but he preferred to act from the point of ostensible defense rather than offense. To achieve these contradictory goals, Hitler ordered the SS to dress up in Polish military uniforms and attack various German border buildings, instill fear in the local German town, and leave behind dead bodies dressed in Polish uniforms. The Nazis simply killed a few dozen concentration camp prisoners and shot them to sell the entire operation as if it were a real Polish attack. The German public was convinced, and the Wehrmacht soon conquered western Poland, with Stalin taking eastern Poland.[38]

How does this relate to the U.S.? Would the U.S. government ever kill Americans in a terrorist act and blame it on a foreign power to provide a pretext for war?

In 1962, the Chairman of the Joint Chiefs, Lyman L. Lemnitzer, proposed Operation Northwoods to President Kennedy. This operation suggested that the U.S. government engage in an array of provocative and illegal actions that would manipulate the American public and world community into supporting the U.S. invasion of Cuba. Among the most traitorous suggestions were the following:

- Blow up a U.S. ship in Guantanamo Bay and blame Cuba
- Develop a communist Cuban terror campaign in the Miami area, in other Florida cities, and even in Washington.

"The terror campaign could be pointed at Cuban refugees seeking haven in the United States. We could sink a boatload of Cubans en route to Florida. We could foster attempts on lives of Cuban refugees in the US even to the extent of wounding in instances to be widely publicized. Exploding a few plastic bombs in carefully chosen spots, the arrest of Cuban agents and the release of prepared documents substantiating Cuban involvement..."[39]

See, some terrorists wear suits and uniforms. I hope this puts to bed any illusions you have about your government. The Joint Chiefs were willing to commit acts of terrorism to achieve a political goal just as Hitler did in 1939. Thankfully, President Kennedy did not approve the plan, but this traitorous general was given ever-increasing responsibility within the U.S. military, an honorable discharge, and is buried with distinction at Arlington National Cemetery. What this tells us is that the U.S. government has no problem committing acts of terrorism to manipulate public opinion.

This brings us to the most consequential event in U.S. history since Pearl Harbor: September 11, 2001.

I do not claim to know the truth of what happened on 9/11, but there is sufficient evidence that casts major questions over the credibility of the official government story. The most shocking part of 9/11 is the fact that most Americans don't truly care who was responsible and find comfort in the official story. This failure to pursue the truth has had devastating consequences. It is one thing to be ignorant of tax policy, but it's a whole different ball game to be ignorant of potential high crimes that endanger the principles of our nation. Too many of us want freedom without responsibility.

That failure to pursue the truth is tragic for our nation, for the men and women who were killed on 9/11, and for the thousands killed in the subsequent wars.

The government's official version of events is that nineteen freedom hating terrorists boarded four planes, crashed two into the Twin Towers, one into the Pentagon, and one in a field in Pennsylvania. As a result of these attacks, the Twin Towers experienced a devastating collapse on national television and, unknown to many, Building 7 of the World Trade Center complex also collapsed later in the afternoon.

Here is the evidence that suggests the official version of events is littered with impossibilities.

1. WTC Building 7 – Asymmetric damage combined with symmetrical collapse at near free fall acceleration

Building 7 was a 47-story office building located one hundred yards north of Tower 1, wasn't hit by an airplane, sustained minor damage from the collapse of Tower 1, and suffered a symmetrical collapse at near free fall acceleration at around 5:20 p.m. on September 11.

The official reason, released by the Department of Commerce's National Institute for Standards & Technology, for the collapse of WTC 7 was that office fires heated the core columns to a high enough temperature causing them to fail and creating a ripple effect that brought down the entire building.

Office fires do not burn hot enough or uniformly enough to cause a total symmetrical collapse of a steel-framed building. When you put your barbeque on and let it heat up to 500 degrees, does the steel crate weaken? It doesn't melt because the melting point of steel is far in excess of temperatures a barbeque can create. The same idea applies to buildings, which is why steel is used. If office fires could completely destroy steel buildings, there would've been numerous building collapses all over the world over the past several decades.

2. WTC Steel Samples that Exhibit Evidence of Vaporization
In a 2002 *New York Times* article entitled "A Search for Clues in Towers' Collapse; Engineers Volunteer to Examine Steel Debris Taken to Scrapyards," the authors remarked:

> "Perhaps the deepest mystery uncovered in the investigation involves extremely thin bits of steel collected from the trade towers and from 7 World Trade Center, a 47-story high rise that also collapsed for unknown reasons. The steel apparently melted away, but no fire in any of the buildings was believed to be hot enough to melt steel outright. A preliminary analysis of the steel at Worcester Polytechnic Institute using electron microscopes suggests that sulfur released during the fires—no one knows from where—may have combined with atoms in the steel to form compounds that melt at lower temperatures."[40]

FEMA addressed this phenomenon in Appendix C of their 2002 report, *World Trade Center Building Performance Study:*

"Two structural steel samples from the WTC site were observed to have unusual erosion patterns. One sample is believed to be from WTC 7 and the other from either WTC 1 or WTC 2.

a. The thinning of the steel occurred by high temperature corrosion due to a combination of oxidation and sulfidation
b. Heating of the steel into a hot corrosive environment approaching 1,800 Fahrenheit results in the formation of a eutectic mixture of iron, oxygen, and sulfur that liquified the steel
c. The sulfidation attack of steel grain boundaries accelerated the corrosion and erosion of the steel

"The severe corrosion and subsequent erosion of Samples 1 and 2 constitute an unusual event. No clear explanation for the source of the sulfur has been identified. The rate of corrosion is also unknown. It is possible that this was the result of long term heating in the ground following the collapse of the buildings. It is also possible that the phenomenon started prior to collapse and accelerated the weakening of the steel structure. A detailed study into the mechanisms of this phenomenon is needed to determine what risk, if any, is presented to existing steel structures exposed to sever and long burning fires."[41]

What these pieces of evidence show is that steel members found at the WTC site exhibited evidence of a sulfidation attack which eroded the steel's strength and may have contributed to the collapse of the Twin Towers and Building 7. The problem with this is that sulfur is not naturally found in offices nor is it magically created by office fires. FEMA admitted they could not identify the source of the sulfur and to this day, no governmental body has submitted a reasonable theory for its existence.

3. Vaporized Materials in WTC Dust Indicating Temperatures Generated Far in Excess of That Generated in Office Fires/Diesel Fuel Fires

In 2003, RJ Lee, a materials characterization laboratory and industrial forensics consulting firm, was hired by Deutche Bank to "evaluate the features of the WTC Dust and WTC Hazardous Substances deposited in the Building as a result of the collapse, ground impact, fires, pressure forces, and other phenomena arising from the WTC Event." In the report, RJ Lee makes a very consequential finding:

> "The amount of energy introduced during the generation of the WTC Dust and the ensuing conflagration caused various components to vaporize. Vapor phase components with high boiling point and high melting point would have, as they cooled, tended to form precipitated particles or thin film deposits on available surfaces through condensation mechanisms. The results of this process would be the presence of a thin layer of deposited material on the surfaces of the dust particulate matter. Many of the materials, such as lead, cadmium, mercury and various organic

compounds, vaporized and then condensed during the WTC Event....The presence of lead oxides on the surface of mineral wool indicates the exposure of high temperatures at which lead would have undergone vaporization, oxidation, and condensation on the surface of mineral wool."[42]

RJ Lee's findings are of monumental importance because they indicate evidence of extreme temperatures not even close to what's possible in a jet fuel aided office fire. Lead does not vaporize until it reaches 3,182 degrees Fahrenheit. This indicates an unknown phenomenon took place during the collapse, a phenomenon that the government has not explained.

4. Eyewitness Testimony of Molten Steel at WTC

Further evidence against the official story was the eyewitness testimony of firefighters, first responders, cleanup professionals, and journalists who reported seeing molten steel at ground zero of the World Trade Center.

Capt. Philip Ruvolo, FDNY explained what he observed at the WTC:

"You get down below and you'd see molten steel— molten steel running down the channel rail, like you're in a foundry, like lava."[43]

Less than two weeks after 9/11, Abolhassan Astaneh, civil engineering professor at the University of California, Berkeley, attempted to study the reasons why the Twin Towers and WTC

7 collapsed. His study was one of eight financed by the National Foundation of Science.

In a PBS documentary, he said "I saw melting of girders in World Trade Center."[44]

On October 2, 2001, the *New York Times* published an article detailing Mr. Astaneh's structural engineering investigation.

The *New York Times* made this statement:

> "Engineers believe they have a general understanding of why the World Trade Center towers fell. Fires stoked by the jetliners' fuel weakened the structural columns. When one floor collapsed, its weight collapsed the floor beneath it, starting a catastrophic series of failures."

And then continued:

> "Dr. Astaneh-Asl and other engineers had assumed that the estimated 310,000 tons of steel columns and beams were being taken to Fresh Kills landfill in Staten Island with the rest of the debris, to be sifted by investigators. **But because the steel provides no clues to the criminal investigation, New York City started sending it to recyclers.**"[45]

How could anyone know for certain how the buildings collapsed without examining the most important evidence: the steel?

> "Dr. Astaneh-Asl's project is one of eight financed by the National Science Foundation to study the World Trade Center disaster. He is also a member of a team

assembled by the American Society of Civil Engineers to investigate the trade center site, and the society is dispatching a team to examine damage to the Pentagon.

One piece Dr. Astaneh-Asl saw was a charred horizontal I-beam from 7 World Trade Center, a 47-story skyscraper that collapsed from fire eight hours after the attacks. The beam, so named because its cross-section looks like a capital I, had clearly endured searing temperatures. Parts of the flat top of the I, once five-eighths of an inch thick, had vaporized."

How could office fires vaporize steel? No one seemed to be asking the simplest questions, while journalists were making wild assumptions and leaps of reasoning unsupported by the evidence.

Again, we are left with the inexplicable: evaporated steel members in a debris pile of the first steel-framed building in history to collapse from office fires.

In 2005, the United States Geological Survey (USGS) released a report detailing the characteristics of the World Trade Center dust. The report, "Particle Atlas of World Trade Center Dust," sought to help with the "identification of WTC dust components."

A FOIA (Freedom of Information Act) request was submitted by two physicists to the USGS to better understand the characteristics of the WTC dust. The USGS complied and provided data that was not previously released to the public. The physicists noted, "The new data demonstrated, significantly, that the USGS team had observed and studied a molybdenum (Mo)-rich spherule..."

The physicists elaborated:

"We discern that considerable study was performed on this Mo-rich spherule, given the number of images and XEDS plots for it, yet these data were not previously released in the public USGS reports.[2] We emphasize these data because of the extremely high melting temperature of molybdenum, and the observation of this molybdenum-rich spherule. Molybdenum is a refractory metal known for its extremely high melting point [9]. Mo melts at 2,623 °C (4,753 °F) [10], although addition of other elements may lower the melting point. No explanation of the high temperature needed to form the observed Mo-rich spherule is given in the USGS material (either published or obtained by FOIA action)..."[46]

In effect, the USGS found evidence that molybdenum melted and solidified in a spherule shape, but the melting point of Mo is 4,753 °F. An office fire could never produce temperature high enough to melt molybdenum, nor could other elements, naturally found at the WTC site, reduce its melting point.

5. Evidence of Foreknowledge by Those Unconnected to Al Qaeda

According to declassified FBI documents, a Union City, New Jersey, resident reported that at 9:00 a.m. on 9/11 five men were filming the Twin Towers burning, clapping, high-fiving, and dancing jovially. These men were arrested days later by Newark police. Their van tested positive for explosive residue. The FBI confirmed the men were Israeli nationals, and at least two were known Israeli intelligence agents. According to additional witnesses, the men were at the New Jersey location across the Hudson River as early as 8:00 a.m.[47] Their actions strongly indicated they had foreknowledge of the attacks and were happy they occurred. If 9/11 was a surprise attack carried out by Al Qaeda, why did Israeli intelligence agents have advance knowledge they would occur? Does that sound like the behavior of innocent men? After being held for nearly three months, the men were deported to Israel, no charges were brought forward, and no further inquiries were made. These men definitely had information of a very material nature, and a true investigation would find out exactly why they were filming the burning Towers with seemingly advance knowledge of the attack.

6. Insider Trading in the Days Before 9/11

Another aspect of 9/11 that must spark questions in an inquisitive mind is the evidence of insider trading in the days before the attacks executed by American institutions on behalf of American clients indicating advance knowledge of the attacks.

In 2004, the Securities and Exchange Commission (SEC) released the statement below regarding suspected 9/11 insider trading:

> "On Sept. 12, 2001, the Securities and Exchange Commission began an investigation to determine whether there was evidence that anyone who had advance knowledge of the terrorist attacks on September 11

sought to profit from that knowledge by trading in United States securities markets. In the course of that review, we did not develop any evidence suggesting that anyone who had advance knowledge of the September 11 attacks traded on the basis of that information...."[48]

Several scientific papers analyzing the trading activity in the days before 9/11 found an extremely high probability that advance knowledge of the 9/11 attacks was used to illegally place stock and option trades that profited off the ramifications. To keep things simple there are two types of options, a call and a put. A call purchase is a bet that the underlying security will increase in price by a given date and a put purchase is the exact opposite bet.

One such academic study was conducted by Professor Marc Chesny of the University of Zurich Department of Banking and Finance, Loriano Mancini Associate Professor of Finance at the Swiss Finance Institute, and UBS analyst Remo Crameri. The study analyzed more than nine million option transactions from the Chicago Board of Exchange, covering thirty-one companies, mainly from the airline, banking, and insurance industries, and spanning from 1996 to 2006. Of the 9.6 million transaction studied, the authors identified thirty-seven option transactions that were, in all probability, insider trading. Of the thirty-seven suspicious transactions found, thirteen occurred in the days before 9/11.

Of the thirteen, ten related to the following airline companies: American Airlines, United Airlines, Boeing, and KLM. American Airlines and United were the two airlines who experienced hijackings on 9/11.[49]

Here's one example: On September 10, 2001, 1,500 American Airlines put contracts with a strike price of $30 expiring in October 2001 were purchased for about $2.15 while the price of America Airlines was $29.75. When the market opened on September 17, 2001, the price of the puts increased from $2.15 to about $12, and the position was sold. On this specific option, there were no trades until about a hundred trades were executed on August 31, 2001, and then about twenty-five to one hundred contracts per day traded from September 4 to September 7. Then, out of nowhere, 1,500 unhedged put options were traded on September 10, giving the buyer the right to sell American Airlines stock for $30 per share. The study's authors put the probability that this was insider trading at 99.8% for three reasons: nonexistent volume in the period preceding the suspicious trades, impeccable timing that led to outsized gains in a matter of days, and no evidence that it was a hedge (a protective as opposed to a speculative bet). The option volume data strongly suggests that the buyer(s) of the puts on September 10 were the seller(s) on September 17, when the markets reopened following the terrorist attacks.

This would be the SEC's easiest insider trading investigation since they could easily find out what brokerage firm executed the trades and discover the identity of the client who placed the trades. To buy 1,500 of these puts on September 10 cost about $322,500 ($215 each), and on September 17, they were worth $1,200 each or $1,800,000, netting a $1.5 million profit in one week.

Evidence of similar insider trading was found in puts purchased on the stocks of:

- Reinsurance companies that were liable to make payouts due to the attacks: Munich Re and the AXA Group
- Financial services companies with offices in or near the Twin Towers: Morgan Stanley, Bank of America, Merrill Lynch, and Citi Group

In addition to the puts purchased on the companies that would lose from the attacks, an abnormal number of calls were purchased immediately preceding 9/11 on Raytheon, a defense contracting company that manufactures tomahawk missiles, among other weapons.

On October 21, 2001, the *San Francisco Chronicle* reported that the SEC had asked for widespread private sector assistance in determining if certain financial transactions before the attacks were due to foreknowledge.

> "On Oct. 2, Canadian securities officials confirmed that the SEC privately had asked North American investment firms to review their records for evidence of trading activity in the shares of 38 companies, suggesting that some buyers and sellers might have had advance knowledge of the attacks. The proposed system, which would go into effect immediately, effectively deputizes hundreds, if not thousands, of key players in the private sector..."[50]

By effectively "deputizing" the private sector, the SEC made it illegal for anyone to publicly disclose anything they learned as a result of analyzing their own firm's trading activity. This effectively ensured secrecy was maintained. A real investigation must lift that secrecy restriction to find out who placed trades with advance knowledge of 9/11.

7. 9/11 Seismic Data

A close study of the seismic data recorded by Columbia University's Lamont-Doherty Earth Observatory (LDEO), located eighteen miles north of Manhattan in Palisades, New York, corroborates the hypothesis that the official version of events is materially incomplete at best. The 9/11 Commission used FAA and NTSB ground radar data, accurate to one second, to ascertain the exact time WTC 1 and WTC 2 were struck by hijacked airplanes. Based on this precise data, the 9/11 Commission determined the time of impact of the North Tower as 8:46:40 and the South Tower as 9:03:11.[51]

The LDEO seismograph located in Palisades, New York, calculated the first seismic waves at 8:46:26 and then again calculated seismic waves emanating from the South Tower at 9:02:54.[52]

These two data sets create a question that has never been investigated, yet potentially invalidates the government's official version of events. Why would a seismograph pick up seismic activity fourteen to seventeen seconds before the airplanes hit the Twin Towers?

Each piece of evidence on its own doesn't prove anything definitively, and there may be perfectly benign explanations for these acute aberrations, but given the extraordinary consequences of 9/11, shouldn't we demand answers to material

We The People Are The Problem

anomalies? If what we were told was not true but we were too lazy to pursue the truth, who is responsible for the ramifications of 9/11? We the People.

It is our civic duty to demand the truth of events that are so important to America and the world. Americans did not seek the truth of 9/11, which is why major questions regarding that day remain unanswered.

If we reflect on society, on human psychology, our culture, and our institutions, it would not be difficult for a well-funded and well-connected group to put in motion a set of events that would lead to the overt destruction of individual rights, the rule of law, and our democratic traditions.

Assuming that the goal of such a group was increasing their own power, politically and economically, they would seek to achieve the following goals with these events:

- The suspension of reason through the invocation of intense fear
- This fear must be intense enough for people to support laws and actions that they otherwise would not support
- This level of fear most efficiently comes from an external enemy that can never be defeated in the traditional sense; hence, the fear is indefinite and the loss of rights and the increased power of the corrupt also indefinite

America has countless urban centers and intense population clusters. These urban centers are extremely dependent on public transportation. If people did not feel safe taking public transportation, entire cities would grind to a halt. That level

Covid 19

63

of fear would give corrupt leaders the ability to take extreme measures that violate our nation's principles but allow the corrupt to pursue their own insidious agenda. Imagine New York City functioning if no one felt safe enough to take the subway to work? What if "terrorists" bombed one New York City subway car every Monday morning for two months? How many people would be taking the subway in New York City? How about across the nation? The police would be forced to turn each subway station into an airport terminal with screenings for all riders. What would rush hour look like in that type of Manhattan? New Yorkers would be throwing their rights into the Hudson River just to take a subway ride in peace. Would people be questioning the attacks themselves and the official version of events reported by the public relations arm of the government? No, they would be fearful, irrational, and ripe for manipulative machinations.

One possible motive to set off terrorist attacks and frighten people into giving up their rights and dignity would be to access their personal lives to gain more control over the population as a whole. What if, in the above scenario, the federal government intervened and offered New Yorkers the ability to access the subway free of police search and to ride the subway with armed soldiers if they gave the government access to their personal lives: recordings of phone calls, text messages, Internet browsing history, products purchased, stores visited, and permanent GPS tracking. The government would call it the "Good Citizen Program," and media pundits would declare, "If you are innocent, you should have nothing to hide." How many people would take the Devil's deal and give up all personal privacy to the government for temporary and illusory security? I posit far more than you can imagine. Taking this scenario further, how could the government use this rich and personal information against their own citizens? It could control people's decision-making and beliefs with far greater effectiveness. Imagine politicians, intelligence agencies, and corporations with access to the daily habits, thoughts, and actions of millions of Americans. It would be Christmas for the corrupt.

This dystopian scenario is actually a reality in China, where by the end of 2020, more than six hundred million cameras will power the Orwellian "Social Credit System," which will monitor each citizen's public actions. You can bet there are Americans in high places who are envious of the Chinese government's surveillance system and would love nothing more than a national crisis to impose a similar system on Americans. This scenario is only possible in America because Americans have repeatedly shown that they do not value the truth, their own freedom, or their hard-earned rights. The enemies of freedom and truth are American citizens who just don't care about anything except their narrow self-interest. These are the debased citizens that demagogues and power thirsty politicians dream of. These people are the root cause of America's decay.

The crimes of the unenlightened wealthy have had extraordinary consequences on their fellow Americans and have led to a palpable decline in the quality of our society.

THE ENLIGHTENED WEALTHY

On the opposite end of the spectrum are the enlightened wealthy—those who believe that wealth is not an end but a means to an end. Those who understand that wealth used for enlightened purposes can transform human society.

The enlightened wealthy understand that they have a responsibility not to give handouts to the lazy and unproductive, not to pander to the uncultured and unmotivated, but to push humanity forward, to reignite the love of truth, of knowledge, and of achievement.

There have been many figures throughout history who have embodied this enlightened ethos and had the power of wealth to amplify their effect on their culture and society.

One of the most shining exemplars of the archetype of the enlightened wealthy was a fifteenth century Florentine banker named Cosimo de' Medici. Cosimo inherited an enormously wealthy family business. Cosimo's father, Giovanni de' Medici, was born a peasant but managed to build a profitable banking business. His bank would be etched into the history books when he made one very lucrative bet with a former pirate who had ambitions of a career in the Catholic Church. Giovanni funded Baldassare Cossa's rise from bishop to cardinal, and then, in 1410, Baldassare Cossa became Pope John XXIII. The former pirate turned Pope did not forget who helped him, and he quickly gave the papal banking business exclusively to the Medici Bank.

This newfound wealth and power put the Medicis at the top of Florentine high society. With this wealth at his disposal, Cosimo would ignite the Italian Renaissance in earnest. The single greatest contribution that Cosimo made was funding the great self-taught architect and engineer, Filippo Brunelleschi, to finish the dome of Florence Cathedral. The cathedral had been unfinished for more than one hundred years because the original builders couldn't determine how to build a self-supporting dome. The recipe for concrete had been lost since the fall of the Roman Empire.

Brunelleschi was an autodidact, teaching himself everything he knew about building. His unconventional thinking gave way to a breakthrough that would lead to one of the greatest architectural achievements in the Western world since the Roman Pantheon.

Brunelleschi figured out how to make the dome self-supporting during the entire building process. He learned how to lift sandstone beams weighing thousands of pounds more than a hundred feet into the sky by ingeniously using oxen, and nearly six hundred years later the Duomo remains the largest masonry dome ever built. The next time you visit Florence and lay your eyes on the great Duomo remember that the genius of Brunelleschi was aided by the wealth of the Medici family, the greatest patrons of the Italian Renaissance.

The wealthy Medici family would not stop funding geniuses. They would go on to sponsor world historical figures, such as Michelangelo Buonarotti, Leonardo Da Vinci, and Galileo Galilei. They would help reignite an interest in the great Ancient Greek philosopher Plato, even funding a Platonic academy and funding the translation of all of Plato's known works. The Medicis made eternal contributions to Western culture by fanning the flames of the Renaissance. They are exemplars of the enlightened wealthy. They show how wealth properly invested can transform cultures and affect people for hundreds of years.

Peter Magistrale

Four days before his fateful ride in Dallas, President Kennedy made a speech to the Florida State Chamber of Commerce. The speech has been largely forgotten, but the end of his speech bears supreme relevance to the subject at hand.

"I realize there are some businessmen who feel that... the balance sheet and profit rate of their own corporation are more important that the worldwide balance of power or the nationwide unemployment rate. But I hope it's not rushing the season to recall to you a passage from Dickens' Christmas Carol, in which Ebenezer Scrooge is terrified by the ghost of his former partner, Jacob Marley. And Scrooge, appalled by Marley's story of ceaseless wandering, cries out: 'But you were always a good man of business Jacob!' And the ghost of Marley, his legs bound by a chain of cash boxes and ledgers, replies: 'Business! Mankind was my business. The common welfare was my business; charity, mercy, forbearance, and benevolence were all my business. The dealings of my trade were but a drop of water in the comprehensive ocean of my business! Members and guests of the Florida State Chamber of Commerce whether we work in the White House or in the State House or in a house of commerce or industry, mankind is our business. And if we can work in harmony instead of hostility, if we can understand each other's problems and position, if we can respect each other's roles and responsibilities, then surely the business of mankind will prosper."[53]

The wealthy must embody the ethos President Kennedy expressed so many years ago and ensure their business dealings are consistent with human decency and enlightened values.

Corrupt Americans will once again attack the foundational principles of our nation. If they succeed, it will be evidence of our own corruption as citizens. We must stand guard and be prepared to defend our nation from the most potent of enemies: internal enemies whose only loyalty is to power and personal enrichment.

In the end, the American elite have put their own economic and political interests ahead of the common good. They have used public education to indoctrinate children with the intention of making them incompetent citizens, emotional consumers, and indifferent to state crimes. They have waged criminal wars of aggression and they have stolen trillions from everyday Americans. If America is to experience an enlightened rebirth the wealthy will need to be held accountable for these crimes and finally adopt a sense of civic duty.

3

THE MIDDLE CLASS INDICTMENT

CULTURE AND VALUES

The middle class must be held accountable for their crimes against America. First is the culture and values of the middle class. Brainwashed by corporate propaganda, the middle class has embraced escapism through entertainment, bliss through ignorance, and happiness through shopping. In the end, consumerism has made the middle class miserable, broke, and empty. Consumer culture is a disgrace to all the Americans who laid the bricks below our feet so that we would not have to walk in the mud. Instead of building pantheons to achievement, we build endless shopping malls.

Their values are an insult to all the soldiers who have died to keep America free. All those young men who died in WWII to defeat the barbarity of the Nazis and the fanaticism of the Japanese would've hoped they died for something more significant than the vain pursuit of materialism. The middle class has embraced consumer culture. This type of lifestyle is built on people always shopping, always spending, and never thinking about the madness of the hamster wheel. The ideals of consumerism are comfort, convenience, and narcissism.

Middle class Americans are so brainwashed by propaganda that they buy things they don't need to impress people they don't like, which is self-destructive and soulless. They don't realize they have been brainwashed to be consumers to create a market that makes producers wealthy. They suffer from the disease of needing instant gratification. What the middle class has done is betray the American tradition of individual freedom and self-sufficiency.

The people of Ancient Rome made a very similar betrayal right before the Roman Republic was destroyed and replaced by Julius Caesar.

Roman poet Juvenal noted the downfall of his countrymen:

"Now that no one buys our votes, the public has long since cast off its cares; the people that once bestowed commands, consulships, legions and all else, now meddles no more and longs eagerly for just two things, bread and circuses."[54]

The middle class of America and the middle class in Caesar's day were cut from the same cloth. They weakened their country by seeking entertainment instead of truth and comfort instead of self-improvement. A republic is doomed to die if its people are this debased. The middle class's profound ignorance on all matters of politics enables the election of corrupt politicians, encourages the looting of the nation's wealth, and empowers criminals to stay in power.

The combination of destroying critical thinking through public school with propaganda from the mainstream media has created a population of ignorant citizens who have repeatedly shown their inadequacy in judging politicians and public affairs. Although they are misinformed, they correctly understand that the economic elites rarely act in their best interest, and the media rarely tells them the truth. It was bad enough when the elites ruled the nation outside of democratic control, but now the situation has metathesized into a lethal combination for democracy: all elites have lost credibility, rightfully so, but the people lack true education thanks to the elite, so their awakening may be a destructive one. The American people may choose a far-right fascist government, like 1930s Germany, or a far-left socialist government, like today's Venezuela. Both possibilities are equally destructive, and both exemplify the shortcomings of American citizens.

The far-right option is possible because people disdain the responsibilities of citizenship and would be happy to defer that responsibility to a strong man figure. The far-right fascists only ask for blind loyalty, which people are already accustomed to, and it requires no extra effort to do so. Thirdly, the far-right fascist offers simple solutions that are often us vs. them, a fictional polarization to garner support for extreme action. This is also natural since people are accustomed to religiously supporting their favorite sports teams and would naturally throw their blind loyalty behind a strong man figure.

The far-left option would be equally destructive. All personal responsibility would be removed from individuals, and the government would be expected to solve all problems. Everyone would be entitled, and no one would be accountable. The productive would subsidize social programs for the unproductive. The college student who takes out $100,000 in student loan debt to attend a private university will be called a victim of the system instead of an irresponsible person who should not be bailed out. The far left ignores that there's inequality of motivation, discipline, and character that factor into the inequality of outcomes. Of course, there is inequality of opportunity, but the vast majority have the basic opportunity to better themselves and improve their lives. They just squander it and look to blame others for their failures. The far-left would seduce Americans with promises of free college, forgiveness of student loan debt, and a universal basic income. Society doesn't work if people are incentivized to be takers instead of producers.

The absence of any sense of civic duty weakens our society and increases the likelihood that the nation gravitates to political extremism. Our leaders used to offer challenges and aspirational goals for the nation. How can any of us forget the iconic words of JFK, "Ask not what your country can do for you but what you can do for your country." The Democratic Party has discarded that ethos. Today, our leaders pander to a narcissistic population like a weak-willed parent panders to their out-of-control teenagers.

People love anyone who will tell them their failures are not their fault and give them something for nothing. Democrats believe that the poor have no responsibility for their failures.

and Republicans think illegal immigrants are the cause of numerous ills across the nation. Democrats completely ignore immigrants who come here poor, not knowing the language, not having an elementary education, not having any connections, and still succeeding. Republicans completely ignore that illegal immigrants take jobs most Americans wouldn't do for more than a month. Both sides ignore the truth because the truth is that individuals are personally responsible for where they are in life, and no one wants to hear that. Too many of us want something for nothing, so the idea of having a duty to society outside a transactional relationship is foreign. This atomizes society and weakens the link between our common humanity. We must develop a new attitude toward our fellow citizens. Instead of seeing people outside our family or friends as irrelevant, we should take a humanistic interest.

IGNORANCE HAS REAL CONSEQUENCES

In New York State, the ignorance of one district is an eye-opening case study. In 2016, I decided to run for the New York State Senate in District 2, located in the North Shore of Long Island and represented by then Senate Majority Leader John Flanagan. Most political issues are not black and white, but one issue that came up during my campaign was an exception to the rule. Up until 2005, New York had a 5-year statute of limitations (SOL) on first-degree rape.

In New York State, a person is guilty of rape in the first degree when:

He or she engages in sexual intercourse with another person[55]:

By "forcible compulsion"—compelling the victim through the use of physical force or the threat of immediate death, physical injury, or kidnapping;

- Who is incapable of consent because of being physically helpless;
- Who is less than 11 years old; or
- Who is less than 13 years old and the defendant is 18 years old or more.

The glaring issue with the SOL on first-degree rape was that most children sexually abused don't come forward until they are well into their twenties and thirties, and therefore the majority of child rapists are never prosecuted.

All of this created a situation where thousands of traumatized children tried to seek justice when they became adults but were unable to do so because the statute of limitations had expired.

In 2005, New York State ended part of this travesty by eliminating the statute of limitations on first-degree rape but only on a go forward basis. All those victims that couldn't come forward before 2005 still had no means of justice.

A small but brave group of child rape victims banded together and lobbied the New York State government to pass a law that allowed victims of first-degree rape before 2005 to press criminal charges.

This law became the Child Victims Act and was passed in the New York State Assembly several times but never came to a vote in the New York State Senate before 2019 because my opponent, the Senate Majority Leader, opposed the bill. When we debated, he argued that people's memories fade, and it would be impossible for the accused to defend themselves in court, hence his opposition. No doubt memories fade, but does a rape victim forget who raped them? That is an insult to our intelligence. The more likely reason Senator Flanagan opposed the Child Victims Act was the fact that powerful religious organizations gave millions to Republicans to vote against the bill. Those campaign contributions kept Republicans in power, and Senator Flanagan needed a Republican majority to remain the Senate Majority Leader. It was simple political calculus. Further evidence of Senator Flanagan's moral bankruptcy was that he voted for the Child Victim's Act in 2019 after the republicans lost their Senate majority and had nothing to gain from opposing the bill. This is a clear as day example of a State Senator only embracing morality when it doesn't conflict with his own power and fundraising ability.

Regardless of party affiliation, though, would any person with a conscience vote for a man who puts personal power before bringing child rapists to justice? More than ninety thousand people voted for such a man in 2016. They were in total ignorance of his shameful policies and voted for him on blind party loyalty, which is destructive to our republic. I can only imagine the thousands of examples like this one where voters were too lazy and too ignorant to know who they were really voting for.

Another example of profound ignorance I experienced while campaigning occurred at a local train station. I decided to hand out pamphlets detailing the facts behind the Child Victims Act to spread awareness. I naively thought, "If only people knew the truth, then they would demand this law be passed." Little did I know that I was about to learn something very important that morning.

Out of the dark and misty air came a tall man about fifty-five years old wearing a black suit. The next train wasn't scheduled to arrive for fifteen minutes, so I decided to introduce myself with the intention of speaking about Senator Flanagan's transgressions surrounding the Child Victims Act. "Good morning. My name is Peter Magistrale. I'm running for the New York State Senate. Did you know New York law protects child rapists?" As soon as he realized I was running for office, his body language got defensive. "Are you running as a Republican or a Democrat?" This wasn't the first time hearing this question on the campaign trail, but it was the first time anyone ignored that I said New York law protects child rapists. I thought that would transcend party loyalty. I responded, "I'm running as a Democrat," but I think the man heard, "I'm running as a Nazi." That would better explain his reaction. "I'm not interested in whatever garbage you are selling. Get lost!" This was the thinking that allowed Senator Flanagan to protect rapists for political gain. I would not stand for it, so I reciprocated by throwing a Molotov cocktail back at him. "Do you support child rapists?" At this point, civility was thrown to the wayside, and we were cursing each other out like a bunch of high school rivals. The situation could've easily escalated to a fistfight, but cooler heads prevailed, and we walked away maintaining only verbal combat.

Of all the people I met while I was campaigning, this man taught me the most. Maybe if it had been 3:00 p.m. we would have been more cordial, but as we know from personal experience, a lack of sleep removes the self-control that oils social situations. He was too tired to lie, and I was too tired to ignore his stupidity. We met in a raw form, and in that raw moment I saw a man imprisoned by ignorance, incapable of even speaking with someone of the opposite political party, and indifferent to the crimes committed by politicians of his "tribe." All this time I was operating under a false assumption: that the politicians were the problem, and if we could change the quality of our leaders, then we could pass bipartisan laws, such as the Child Victims Act. That assumption completely ignored why criminal politicians were being elected in the first place. It all crystallized that cold morning in October 2016.

The corrupt get reelected because the people are profoundly ignorant and easily manipulated. The politicians aren't the problem. The people are the problem. The middle class elects American leaders. The poor and rich are demographic minorities even in voter turnout.

If the middle class is largely responsible for electing corrupt politicians, what does that say about them? It proves ignorance of the truth, misplaced loyalty, and blind obedience to corrupt political parties. Party allegiance is irrational because no party holds a monopoly on good ideas, and only through the dialectic of disagreement are laws perfected. Middle class Americans fall far short of their responsibilities as citizens, and the thousands of free rapists in New York are emblematic of this failure.

BLIND LOYALTY TO POLITICAL PARTIES

Of the many civic vices of American life, none is more dangerous than the blind loyalty people have toward their political party of choice. There are many people who have voted for candidates of the same party their whole lives. This empowers career politicians who use their unchecked power to enrich themselves. Why do people have loyalty to the corrupt? They think supporting "their" political party is like supporting their favorite football team. For some odd reason, their identity is tied to political parties. Once this occurs, the emotional centers control the political opinions of citizens. Any evidence that your party or candidate is inferior, unqualified, or hopelessly corrupt is ignored. The only thing that matters is that my guy wins or the opposing party loses. We treat politics like a high school prom, Super Bowl, or beauty contest, and then we wonder why we have atrocious leaders. Is the answer not yet clear? We have incompetent citizens.

Strip your political loyalties and be loyal only to your principles and values. Americans must value truth, must pursue it, and must then use that knowledge to make more informed decisions as citizens. Unfortunately, everything about human nature makes the pursuit of truth unlikely. The truth is foreign to most people because they make decisions with feelings instead of logic. What is right or wrong depends on how it makes them feel. A demagogue knows how to capitalize on this flaw of judgment.

Does the democratic establishment really care about the urban poor they ostensibly champion? Fifty-five years after the Great Society policies were declared by Lyndon Johnson society remains status quo for the poor. Regardless of their intentions, Democrats have spent trillions trying to end poverty and failed because they ignored human nature. The Democratic Party has pandered to obscure minorities and ignored the structural issues facing the entire nation. They have engaged in gender politics, pitting men versus women to get the female vote. While they debate how many genders exist in the human race, wars persist, corruption multiplies, and high crimes go unpunished.

Does the Republican establishment really care about the blue-collar workers from Middle America? Republican politicians, through anti-union and pro-corporation legislation, have helped destroy the American middle class.

The Republican Party of Teddy Roosevelt and the Democratic Party of FDR and JFK are long gone. All elements of moderation, pragmatism, and rationality within the parties have been marginalized and replaced by the unrealistic, the simplistic, and the irrational. First came Obama. He overpromised and underdelivered. Then the American people were given the impossible choice between the most corrupt of politicians and the most debased and primitive of businessmen. The corruption of the major political parties, empowered by voter apathy and ignorance, has created an ever-growing opening for demagogues to exploit. Unless Americans become competent citizens, they will be ripe for the taking. Politicians will pander to voter fears and dreams, create false enemies to blame their problems on, and manipulate emotions to gain support.

You would think the urban poor and blue-collar workers, the stalwarts of the Democratic and Republican parties, respectively, would question their blind loyalty due to the lack of results they are getting from their preferred parties. Voting habits prove otherwise. The Democratic Party is supposed to be the party of the poor, yet Lyndon Johnson's Great Society policies have spent $22 trillion since 1964 with no discernable impact on poverty.[56] Blue-collar workers voted for politicians who destroyed their unions and outsourced their jobs. Both ends of the political spectrum have failed to honestly evaluate the results they've received from their tribe. These are the results of a misplaced loyalty that has destructive consequences on our society. No party or politician can be beyond critical analysis.

Elections must become meritocracies of leadership and capability, not vain popularity contests where votes are harvested with bribes.

AMERICAN SOCIETY IS BASED ON IGNORANCE

The most important parts of American society are based on ignorance. Ignorant voters, ignorant consumers, and ignorant citizens create an all-around ignorant society. Ignorance is oil for wage slavery, state crimes, propaganda, and all the other control mechanisms put in place by those at the top of society. In our crony capitalist society, ignorance is of supreme importance to the most powerful people. Politicians need it to be reelected, the defense industry needs it to keep siphoning tax dollars, corporations need it to sell their latest gadgets free from critical eyes, academics need it to keep their cushy jobs teaching half-truths, the entertainment industry needs it so that people can waste their time and money getting lost in illusions and fantasy, every religion needs it to steal their followers' money, and the media needs it to tell shameless lies to get the attention needed to sell ads.

The American who shows a distaste for civic responsibility and whose great aim in life is comfort and ease is a greater threat to America than any bomb could be. The American who mindlessly chants, "USA! USA! USA!" when a politician wraps themselves in the flag permits the highest of crimes. The American who votes out of extreme ignorance for the politicians who steal, lie, and cheat should share a cell with the criminals they empower. The American who knows more about pop culture than politics harms America. We must demand more from ourselves and each other.

Ignorant citizens do far greater damage to our society than any terrorist. The irony is striking.

Why are ignorant Americans more dangerous than Middle Eastern terrorists? Ignorant Americans vote for selfish, corrupt, and ignorant leaders. These leaders then have access to the world's most powerful military, spying apparatus, and hundreds of billions of dollars in federal tax revenue.

We invest this power not with the most·enlightened among us, but the most ruthless. The military is used to protect the profits of corporations, while the worth of a soldier's life is not included in the calculus. Our leaders wholeheartedly believe that in the pursuit of power and wealth human life, human rights, and human decency are dispensable. We elect leaders who earmark our tax dollars for wars of profit, and then use the immense resources of the intelligence community to spy on innocent Americans. If people elect a criminal government, are they not responsible for

We The People Are The Problem

the crimes of that government? So many of us place the blame of the Holocaust partially on the German people who voted the Nazi Party into power, but who blames Americans for the thousands of American soldiers killed in the illegal Iraq War and the war's collateral damage, which killed hundreds of thousands of Iraqi citizens? Where is our sense of responsibility? We have none, but we are no less culpable for the crimes committed in our names by the leaders we empower.

As citizens of the most powerful and most important country on earth, we must reflect on our shortcomings, the damage those shortcomings have inflicted on the world and our society, and how we can improve ourselves.

If we as a nation want to change, then we must recognize that the change must first occur in our hearts and minds.

As citizens, we have duties, not to the state itself, but to human fellowship.

If we want to improve America, we must embrace our duties as Americans:

- Remove the corrupt from their high places in government, religion, academia, the military, and corporate America
- Pledge loyalty only to your conscience, the pursuit of truth, and the greater good
- Cease living according to the dictates of propaganda and self-direct your life
- In all matters of life, produce more than you consume
- Reject the easy, purposeless, and vacuous things our society tempts you with and pursue the purposeful and the transformative

- If fear motivates you, then fear ignorance, personal stagnation, and dying before achieving your purpose in life
- Commit to autodidactic learning about history, society, culture, and all knowledge that allows us to make better decisions today
- Acknowledge the corrupt and then stop giving them power, which means stop voting for them, stop admiring them, and stop buying their products

CIVIC DUTY AND COVID-19

The COVID-19 pandemic has brought out the best and the worst in American civic life. The reprehensible actions of the Chinese government to not release the full facts of the deadly virus afflicting their nation allowed the pandemic to become a worldwide phenomenon. President Trump did not contribute to the solution when he initially downplayed the threat as a hoax meant to hurt his reelection chances. Early inaction on the part of the federal and state governments meant that America would face a much more severe outbreak than a country that took proper measures immediately, like South Korea.

Aside from what the president should or should not have done, the American people have largely used common sense and abided by social distancing rules. When we look back on how America got through this pandemic, the government will not be thanked, but the frontline workers, the doctors, nurses, and delivery people will be recognized as heroes for saving countless lives and transporting critical goods in a time of crisis. Aside from the federal government, another group that history will not look kindly on are those whose selfishness and ignorance has inspired them to protest social distancing and the shutdown of the economy.

On April 15, 2020, gun wielding, Confederate flag waving, far-right protesters descended on the Michigan state capitol and protested the governor's social distancing orders. They compared the Michigan governor, Gretchen Whitmer, to Hitler and the Nazis, holding signs saying "Heil Whitmer" and suggesting the governor was a tyrant who should be hanged. The protest was organized by conservative organizations funded by far-right billionaires, such as the Koch and DeVos families—billionaires who have loyalty only to their own economic interests and not the common good of society.

What did the protesters want? One protestor was nearly in tears because he couldn't buy fertilizer or grass seed. Another mindless protestor was upset that her gray roots were growing out and that she couldn't get her hair dyed. The topping on the cake of this festival of ignorance were protesters who compared social distancing policies with the totalitarianism of communist China. One protestor told Fox News, "I hope Whitmer understands she's not going to be able to rule Michigan like other politicians rule China..." Another protestor held up a sign saying "Social Distancing = Communism." This is ignorance at the highest level since social distancing saves lives, and they would prefer people die needlessly in order to preserve their consumer impulses.

I'd like to think this level of ignorance is isolated to the fringe of American society, but there were similar protests in North Carolina, Kentucky, New York, California, Louisiana, Florida, Texas, Pennsylvania, Washington, Indiana, New

Hampshire, Maryland, and Colorado. To think these protesters are on the fringe of American society would be ignoring the virus that has permeated so many Americans.

These protesters are symptomatic of an ever-growing number of Americans who not only do not have any sense of civic duty but have also lost touch with reality. Their actions are proof that ignorance and selfishness have a strong foundation in the depths of American civic life.

During World War II, Americans had to make sacrifices for the greater good. That meant men enlisting in the military and women contributing to war manufacturing. Do you think people were thrilled about the immediate realities? I doubt it, but they stepped up and fulfilled their duties. They didn't protest their freedoms were being taken away or that they had a right to defy the obvious common good.

Another example of an acceptable and necessary trade-off between safety and freedom are traffic lights. The lights serve to protect all motorists, but to do so everyone must stop at a red light from time to time. Do people protest red lights because it temporarily impedes their freedom of movement?

People who are selfish and ignorant to the point they are willing to allow their fellow Americans to die from an avoidable death are an embarrassment to America.

True Patriotism

Nothing that is wrong with America is outside the control of Americans. We must take personal responsibility for the criminals we empower, the corrupt we support, and the truth we ignore. Once we take responsibility, we put the power back in our hands. Improvement comes from acknowledging an unacceptable condition and using that knowledge as motivation to change for the better. We need to know how bad we've been so that we can be motivated to be better.

If we live true to these duties, the republic will be made stronger, and the human race's future will be made much brighter. Let us not wait for the eleventh hour for a Caesar to guillotine our republic. Let us learn from antiquity. Let us learn from the Caesars of Ancient Rome and the demagogues of Ancient Greece. Tyrants rise when the quality of the citizenry drops to a hopeless level. Our quality is dropping fast as evidenced by the mirror on our soul that is our politics and culture. The decay of our society is a reflection of our decay as citizens. We are derelict in our duties, but we can change.

A true patriot knows patriotism has nothing to do with waving a flag but protecting what that flag represents and knowing that our greatest enemies are Americans who pursue power at the expense of our freedoms and human decency.

Who has done more damage to America: the criminals who occupy the highest places of American society or the boogey men we are told to be afraid of? The enemies within have done far more damage than any external enemies.

EQUALITY IS A MYTH

There is some semblance of equality before the law and equality of opportunity, but there will never be equality of quality. Some people are more artistic than others, while some are more athletic. Human beings are as varied in talent and competence as each grain of sand on a beach. In all matters, except politics, we make distinctions and award honors and responsibilities, more or less, on each individual's proven ability. Only a small fraction of society are doctors, surgeons, or anesthesiologists because only a small fraction has the will, financial resources, and innate ability to become competent in these complex fields. If your child's life were on the line and you needed the best heart surgeon to save their life, would you ask an electrician to perform the surgery or the best heart surgeon with decades of experience successfully performing the sort of surgery your child needs? Herein lies the weakness of democracy: we assign equality where equality does not exist. We give equal weight to the opinion of the ignorant and the opinion of the knowledgeable. The solution is to raise the broad knowledge and awareness of the citizenry as a whole. The solution resides in giving each citizen a ruler's education and instilling in them republican values.

RULER'S EDUCATION

What is a ruler's education, and what are republican values?

First, a ruler's education is centered around bestowing intellectual weapons to defeat amoral politicians, corporate con men, and insidious propaganda.

How can we help people protect themselves and consequently our society from those who deceive, manipulate, and destroy for their personal gain? First, Americans need to recognize that they have been deliberately dumbed down by the many tools available to the nation's economic elite, including public education and the media. Everything they have heard on television needs to be scrutinized, new cultural norms are needed, and the very meaning of being American has to be reformed.

We The People Are The Problem

Here are the most important lessons people can apply to their daily lives that would reform the United States instantly:

1. Loyalty to authority should be reserved for those who have earned it, subject to ongoing review.
2. Blind obedience is the ideal of a slave.
3. The purpose of public education is to make compliant wage slaves, ignorant citizens, and emotional consumerists.
4. Give yourself a noble purpose in life.
5. Value excellence in every aspect of your life.
6. Seek knowledge over entertainment, seek truth over convenient myths, seek the purposeful over the vacuous.
7. Life is short; live according to your conscience.
8. The unexamined life is a tragedy.

Republican values have nothing to do with the Republican Party but rather the values that will protect the posterity of our republic.

1. Each citizen has a duty to contribute to their community and their nation.
2. Each citizen has a duty to protect their society from those who have given in to human weakness and embraced corruption in all its forms.
3. The outcome of each person's life is of supreme importance.
4. Truth, knowledge, and wisdom must guide our lives and decision-making.

Peter Magistrale

An Enlightened Culture

The aspects of our culture that do not serve enlightened ends and human well-being must be discarded. This means the end of consumerism, worshipping celebrities, and blind patriotism. All three of these phenomena are manifestations of ignorance. Consumerism functions under the assumption that you need what some corporation is selling, that you need to compete with your peers to have the nicest things, and that your possessions define you. Nothing could be further from the truth. What human beings need more than anything external is internal peace. A peace that comes from knowing you are living according to your conscience and your life purpose. No physical thing can do for humanity what humanity must do for itself. We must choose to live nobly with purpose, excellence, and courage. Our purpose in life should guide our decisions and actions, not our fleeting appetites or carnal desires. It is these primitive aspects of our psyche that gravitate to the false charisma and unrealistic promises of demagogues. It's the love of ease and pleasure that corrupts our character and civic duty.

If we seek to have a citizenry that can effectively elevate the most enlightened leaders and ostracize the most unenlightened, then each citizen must be taught the psychology of the unenlightened and how they have gained power the world over. With this knowledge, the common man can defend himself against the propaganda and deception that currently empowers the corrupt. How does a corrupt corporate executive or an amoral politician view the world? To understand those in high places who use their power for corrupt ends, one must understand the psychological dark triad: psychopathy, narcissism, and Machiavellianism.

A psychopath is an apex predator of the human realm. Their psychological makeup is optimized for gaining power. They lack compassion for others, and they do not allow morality to impede their objectives. To a psychopath, the end always justifies the means. Politics is the playground of psychopaths.

Narcissism is a manifestation of an excessive and unhealthy love of self. At its core is an insecurity that is masked by a faux self-confidence and false bravado. A narcissist has no compassion for his fellow man because he's not at peace with himself. The narcissist is a disastrous leader whose excessive pride blinds his decision-making and lack of compassion aids in callous disregard for the well-being of human beings.

The leader of Machiavellian makeup is dangerous because their true motives are so well concealed. No one is truly aware of who they are dealing with and empowering. The human chameleon is a dangerous creature in a free society. They are poison inserted into the body politic by the ignorance and naivete of their fellows. The Machiavellian figure is prone to demagoguery and can intuit what crowds want to hear and what buttons to push to manipulate their decision-making.

Anyone who can sway a crowd in a democracy is a powerful force. The crowd is not rational, not reflective, and poor judges of good leaders. Can an enlightened leader sway an unenlightened crowd? Can an unenlightened leader sway an enlightened crowd? The answer is no on both accounts. What is intriguing to contemplate is the overwhelming likelihood that the American citizenry is the most dangerous force on earth. Powerful, but ignorant, we allow criminals to control the most powerful force on earth. Criminals occupy positions of power because we are so easily swayed by those who tell us our problems are not our fault, our enemies are external, and our freedom is under attack. How far would a politician get telling the U.S. population the truth: their ignorance is 100% responsible for their problems, our greatest enemies are corrupt Americans, and our freedom is under attack by those whose power is inversely correlated to our freedom. We need to stop thinking in binary simplistic terms. We need to understand how those in power use our ignorance of political affairs and human nature to commit acts that defy our nation's constitution and our founding principles. Stop thinking that all Americans love America just because they wrap themselves in the flag. The most powerful see this nation as no more than a stepping-stone for personal ambition. The most corrupt have no problem killing Americans, poisoning your food, destroying your environment, and outsourcing your job if this can make them richer in the process.

Taxing Civic Ignorance

The easiest way to protect America from the psychopaths who love power and the ambitious devoid of good judgment is to enlighten the People to the importance of America, the fragility of our republic, and their obligation as citizens to protect our nation from the multitude of internal enemies.

Being a competent citizen is just as difficult as becoming competent in any other worthwhile endeavor except that widespread citizen incompetence is far more dangerous than any professional incompetence. If a civil engineer is incompetent, it may lead to the collapse of a bridge, but the bridge can be rebuilt. Once a republic dies, it cannot be rebuilt.

How can we become more capable citizens who elect the wisest, disempower the unenlightened, and ensure America's power is used to achieve enlightened ends? American apathy and ignorance of domestic political affairs is infamous. It's about time we gave people a good reason to be knowledgeable citizens.

To that end, I propose a federal and state tax on civic ignorance and a tax credit for demonstrable civic knowledge.

To file your federal tax return each year, you would take a reasonably timed multiple choice civics exam addressing American history, how laws are made, the role of the three branches, the U.S. Constitution, and current public officials. Each question would be reasonably timed to limit cheating, and results would be shown after completing the test. Based on your score, you could get a tax credit or owe more tax. The tax would be adjusted for income and age and operate on a sliding scale with 75% being a passing grade.

The groups below would be exempt from paying a tax if they failed:

- Anyone making below $50,000 for a single person and $100,000 for married or head of household
- Anyone under the age of 18 or over the age of 65
- Anyone with a medically diagnosed disability or disease

The tax credit, as a percentage of income, would be greatest the younger you are, the lower your income, and the higher your score.

The tax for failing, as a percentage of income, would be greatest the older you are, the more income you make, and the lower your score.

The reason for this inversion is to address the prolific ignorance of young people and give them a real incentive to change their behavior and on the opposite end to change the behavior of people who have gotten older and wealthier but not wiser. The reasoning goes the older you are, the more life experience you have and the wiser you should be; therefore, ignorance of civic obligations is less forgivable. The young have many natural reasons for being ignorant, but if they can be incentivized to take their obligation as citizens seriously, it would be the greatest return on investment.

Additionally, the poor would not be taxed for failing, but they would be eligible to receive a tax credit for a passing grade, thus providing a win-win opportunity for people of modest means to receive extra income for demonstrating they are knowledgeable citizens.

Third, anyone making more than $250,000 for a single person or $500,000 for married or head of household would not receive a tax credit for passing but would still be assessed a tax for failing.

Fourth, if an elected official fails the civics exam, they will be forced to step down at the conclusion of their current term.

Fifth, anyone who fails the annual civics exam would be precluded from running for public office for three years.

The above is aimed at the federal level, but the same set of civics tax laws can be instituted at the state and local level as well. The test would be administered before submitting the state tax return (excluding states without a state income tax), would cover state-level civics, and would affect the state tax owed.

In addition to incentivizing knowledge of civics, we should also incentivize upstanding citizens to participate in volunteer programs that have demonstrable public benefits.

Big Brothers Big Sisters is a tremendous American nonprofit organization that facilitates mentorship programs for all children whose parents seek a positive mentor in their child's life. They match volunteer mentors with children from troubled backgrounds. Mentors (Bigs) spend anywhere from three to five hours per month with their assigned mentee (little) doing a variety of low-cost activities with the humble goal of building a healthy positive relationship with each other.

This simple program, which doesn't require anything extraordinary except a desire to uplift a child, has proven to have exceptional results on the future of at-risk children.

Academic studies and common sense show that a child who is at risk of being left behind in life is less likely to do drugs and commit crimes when they have an adult mentor they can emulate and depend on. For every child who is positively affected not to commit a crime as an adult, society at large saves more than $1 million. This is based on the average cost of incarceration being $33,000 per year across the U.S. (in 2015),[57] social cost of incarceration being 10x the incarceration cost,[58] and the average sentence being 3.3 years.[59]

Ignorance cannot be legislated out of existence, but it must be disincentivized to the fullest extent. People may be ignorant for many reasons, but, as a society, we must make a decision to reject ignorance and ostracize those who embrace folly.

As the great Athenian statesman Pericles once said:

"We do not regard a man who takes no interest in public affairs as harmless. We do not say that such a man 'minds his own business.' Rather we say he has no business here at all."[60]

Our republic only works if the People seek the truth of politics and government and fight for the ideals of our nation. We cannot afford to be a nation of willfully ignorant, self-interested mindless consumers and expect our nation to survive in its current form. Again, the greatest threat to America is ignorant Americans of all socioeconomic backgrounds.

When I decided to run for the New York State Senate in 2016, I met with the local party leader to get his endorsement. Our conversation was illuminating. He asked me what my platform would be, and I told him I wanted to strengthen campaign finance laws, eliminate the carried interest loophole, and pass the Child Victim's Act. When I was done speaking, he responded memorably: "Only a small minority of people will vote for you based on your stance on issues. The vast majority will vote for you based on your youthful looks or some other vain attribute." As I campaigned and knocked on doors, his prophecy came true. One particular morning stands out. It was a bright sunny Saturday morning in June, and I had my clipboard that held a list of registered Democrats in that neighborhood. I needed to get a thousand signatures to qualify for the ballot in November. I walked up to the first home and rang the bell. An older woman answered the door. I introduced myself, told her I was a Democrat running for the New York State Senate, and asked her to sign her name to help me qualify for the November election. She ignored everything I said and responded by saying: "You're so cute!" and pinched one of my cheeks. She proceeded to playfully flirt with me, but I focused her attention back on why I had knocked on her door. In the end, she signed my petition but hardly because of my stance on issues. I remember walking away thinking if this lady is the norm we are screwed.

After months of campaigning and having people slowly erode my confidence in them, one man did surprise me. It was late in the afternoon on a brisk fall day close to election day 2016. He was sitting with his wife on the front porch. I introduced myself, and we started taking about state politics. He then said, "I have a question for you. Of all the people I have asked this question, only two people have answered it correctly. What is the thing that is equal among all people?" I pondered for a moment and responded, "We are all mortal." He was pleasantly surprised that a young aspiring politician had awareness of human mortality. I was rejuvenated to be talking about a fundamental human reality. Politics, or so I thought, was supposed to be about improving the human condition through rational laws that help people achieve their potential before the inevitable day of departure comes. I doubt many people I encountered on the campaign trail would entertain such a thought. During my campaign, I knocked on hundreds of doors and spoke to no more than two thousand people in total, my website had a few thousand hits, if that, yet I received nearly forty-eight thousand votes. More than 90 percent of the people that voted for me had no idea who I was or what I stood for. My opponent received approximately 92,000 votes, and I would argue that 90 percent voted blindly for him as well. How can we have honest, qualified leaders if people are incompetent when it comes to choosing leaders? How is it not obvious to everyone that Americans are enabling the corrupt politicians who are destroying America?

The Cost of Ignorance

Ignorance has very real consequences, financially as well as politically. Here's one example of the financial cost of ignorance to the average American: Going to a college that you can't afford instead of a state school for one-fourth the price and equal quality.

In 2019, the average annual public college tuition after aid and scholarships was approximately $4,000, while the average tuition for private colleges after aid and scholarships was about $15,000.[61] Over four years, the difference is $44,000. In most cases, public universities are perfectly good substitutes to overpriced private universities. Let's say the average 18-year-old chooses to major in accounting and has the choice between equally reputable private and public universities. Further, let's assume they choose the private option, graduate in four years, take out a student loan for $11,000 each year, and begin repaying the loan at age twenty-two with an interest rate of 5% due over the next ten years. Lastly, let's assume that attending a private university is not a causal factor in determining their current and future earnings power.

A summary of the loan would be as follows:

Year	Loan Taken	Accrued Interest	Total Debt
Freshman	$11,000	$2,371	$13,371
Sophomore	$11,000	$1,734	$12,734
Junior	$11,000	$1,128	$12,128
Senior	$11,000	$550	$11,550
Total	**$44,000**	**$5,783**	**$49,783**

The above reflects interest compounding annually to make the calculation simpler. On January 1 of year 5, the student has a debt totaling $49,783 that is due over the next ten years with a 5% compounding interest rate. The student will make 120 monthly payments of $528, making the ultimate incremental cost of private university $63,360, assuming the loan isn't paid off early. If that same student had taken the public university route, they would be able to save $528 more per month for ten years. How much money would that grow to be if the student, in the alternative scenario, went to public university and invested $528 each month in a low-cost total stock market index fund and earned a 7% annual rate of return? In ten years, they would have a portfolio worth $91,389.

If the former public university student kept the portfolio invested for the next thirty years until they retired, earned 5% after inflation and fees, the portfolio would be worth $394,978. The power of compounding returns dictates that ignorant financial decisions made in determining which college to attend can have disastrous consequences on your future wealth and well-being. In this scenario, the difference in after inflation wealth in forty years was more than $400,000. That all comes from an ill-informed decision made at eighteen. The cost of ignorance is real and measurable.

	Private University	**Public University**	**Difference**
Cost per year	$15,000	$4,000	$11,000
Cost of Loan Taken	$44,000	-	$44,000
Effect on Net Worth in 10 years	($44,000)	$91,389	$135,389
Effect on Net Worth in 40 years	($44,000)	$394,978	$438,978

Another key point is that people must take personal responsibility for the decisions they make that shape their life. If someone has a hard time paying their bills after choosing to finance the cost of their private college education, does the public owe them a bailout for their short-sighted decisions? Should their student loans be forgiven? Responsible people should not bail out irresponsible people, regardless of whether it's a Wall Street investment bank or a college student. Forget about society for a moment and focus on your own family. Are there people in your family who are terrible with money? Would they be better off if someone just handed them money or taught them how to manage and value money? We must help people help themselves. Ironically, this is what Democrats believed before Lyndon Johnson's Great Society policies. As much as parents are tempted to do everything for their children, they would be wise to think about how their actions, no matter how pure their intentions, affect their children. Everything a parent does should be done with this question in mind: "How will this affect my child's character in the long run?" Too many of us fail to understand human nature. If you do everything for your children, there's nothing left for them to do, and they never gain personal life competence. They never encounter challenges that would otherwise give them the self-confidence and grit needed to pursue excellence. What happens when the government makes people believe they are entitled to assistance? They never become independent or productive members of society. Worst of all is that they never reach their full potential as human beings.

Middle Class Heroes

Who are the heroes of the middle class? Their heroes are people such as Kim Kardashian, LeBron James, and Gisele Bündchen. Is it enlightened to worship vacuous celebrities, inconsequential sports stars, and talentless models? By doing this, the middle class degrades our nation culturally. They feed our unsatisfying intellectually dead celebrity culture, which turns people toward the vain and trivial instead of the pursuit of truth and societal advancement. What is a sports star without fans? What is a celebrity without followers? What is a model without insecure people? Nothing at all. These people offer little value to society yet are held up as our heroes. When young people idolize narcissistic attention whores with no talent, how does that affect them? Those we consider our heroes have grave consequences for the whole of society. When we celebrate the arrested development in the famous and influential, we invite the same defects onto young impressionable minds.

Take a step back. Put down your national identity and the traditions you are supposed to follow and think for a moment how insane it is that eighty thousand people spend four hours each to go to a football stadium to watch the Super Bowl and support people who will never have any effect on their lives. In one night, the spectacle consumes 320,000 hours from fans in attendance, and no matter the outcome of the game, two things are certain: 1) millions of Americans will know every side effect of Viagra, and 2) everyone will return to the unenlightened world we call home.

Mass sports entertainment is about escape. It's about people escaping their drudgery for several hours. It's a collective act of cowardice because instead of architecting an escape from our prison, we architect an escape from reality. This embrace of the inconsequential only perpetuates our imprisonment.

Sports stars can only be paid millions because fans are in the stands. The only reason modeling is a profession is because there's insecurity to be exploited for profit. Models such as Gisele are useless parasites that profit off human weakness. She has a twin sister who isn't nearly as beautiful as she is, hence isn't a supermodel. Both women are products of the same parents except one hit the genetic lottery. Being physically attractive is not an achievement; it produces nothing; it helps no one. Celebrities have clout because people worship them religiously. What's the common denominator in these power dynamics?

These people have unjustifiable wealth and prestige because we grant it to them. The moment we restructure our value system and appraise their real contribution to furthering society their power will evaporate instantly. Here's the accurate measure of any profession: if everyone in your profession suddenly quit, what effect would it have on society? If police officers went on strike, mayhem would ensue. If doctors and nurses went on strike, hospitals would become hotels for the ill to die. Now think what would happen if sports stars went on strike. Absolutely nothing besides the sentimental and emotional value lost from people not being able to root for their favorite teams. What would happen if celebrities and models didn't show up for work? If they couldn't sell their looks, they'd probably be homeless, but other than that the world would not miss them at all. If we are to increase our quality as a nation, the middle class must discard the false idols and revalue all values.

In the end, the middle class is responsible for electing the criminals that run America, supporting a soulless consumer culture, and betraying the foundational principles of our republic, but all of this can change if the middle class adopts a more enlightened value system and lives up to their civic duty.

4

WHAT AMERICANS CAN LEARN FROM ANCIENT ROME

The failure of the Ancient Roman Republic teaches us to reexamine our values and ensure that civic virtue takes priority over unrestrained personal ambition and destructive narcissism.

The Roman Republic was destroyed by the pernicious deterioration of Roman character. Julius Caesar did not destroy Rome. Romans did. The citizens of Rome went from preferring death to dishonor to preferring bread and circuses over civic duty.

Ancient Rome rose to prominence because its society was based on a currency that incentivized virtue. The currency was honor, and it was distributed based on the actions one took to advance the interests of the Roman Republic.

THE VIRTUE OF APPIUS CLAUDIUS

This ethos is epitomized in a profound speech delivered by a blind Roman senator named Appius Claudius. In 280 B.C., the Greek King Pyrrhus of Epirus came to the defense of its Greek ally, Tarentum, located in southern Italy. He amassed a force of professional infantryman, cavalry, and elephants and invaded southern Italy with the intention of diffusing the growing threat that was the Roman Republic. When Pyrrhus met the Romans in open combat, he was surprised how formidable they were, remarking, "...the discipline of these barbarians is not barbarous."[62] Although the Greeks were victorious in their first battle, they had suffered irreplaceable losses in manpower. To end the conflict before things deteriorated further, Pyrrhus sent an offer of peace to the Romans if they agreed to relinquish their domination of the Greek cities in southern Italy. The peace offer was delivered by a persuasive Greek diplomat named Cineas of Thessaly.

Cineas went to Rome with gifts for Roman senators and lenient terms. Pyrrhus' terms were on the verge of senatorial approval until Appius Claudius was carried into the senate house by his sons. Old age and blindness had, until now, kept him out of public activities, but he refused to allow the senate to vote before he was heard. In the senate house, Appius Claudius stood up and berated his fellow Romans for entertaining a treaty that would only weaken them:

> "Up to this time, O Romans, I have regarded the misfortune to my eyes as an affliction, but I now wish I was deaf as well as blind, so I would not hear the shameful resolutions which bring low the glory of Rome."

The senators quickly understood that accepting Pyrrhus' offer threatened Rome's posterity. Even though each senator could have accepted the gifts that accompanied Pyrrhus' emissary, they rejected them because their honor and the survival of Rome were more important. They put the interests of Rome before their own because honor meant more than personal wealth. How many Americans would put the common good over their desire to accumulate wealth?

The Virtue of Gaius Fabricus Luscinus

Another example of the early Roman Republic's exceptional citizenry occurred shortly after Appius Claudius' scolding speech in the senate. Pyrrhus had taken numerous Roman prisoners over the course of several successful battles. The Roman senate dispatched Gaius Fabricus Luscinus, not to negotiate peace, but to negotiate the release of the Romans being held prisoner by Pyrrhus. Upon hearing that a Roman embassy was headed to negotiate, Pyrrhus assumed they were coming to negotiate a peace treaty. He also learned from his fellow countryman Cineas that Fabricus was a man of high standing in Roman society but not wealthy. Pyrrhus attempted to bribe Fabricus with an enormous amount of gold and make him the wealthiest man in Rome. Fabricus refused the bribe because he embodied the ideals of the Roman Republic. Pyrrhus was so impressed with the incorruptibility of Gaius Fabricus that he released the Roman prisoners without negotiation. Roman society honored those who made great contributions to the Roman commonwealth. Pyrrhus' bribe failed because he failed to realize that the most important currency in Roman society was the honor distributed based on merit to those whose achievements contributed to the greater glory of the

Roman Republic. This currency was controlled exclusively by the Roman state, and any Roman who accepted a bribe would destroy their good name.

Roman Virtue During the First Punic War

The third example of exceptional character displayed by the citizens of the early Roman Republic occurred during the first Punic war between Rome and Carthage. The war began in 264 B.C. and pitted a regional land-based Roman power against a formidable seafaring foe that controlled the strategic island of Sicily and had the most powerful navy in the western Mediterranean. Rome would wage a war of attrition fought mostly on the island of Sicily and the surrounding sea. After twenty-three years of fighting, Rome and Carthage were on the brink of bankruptcy, and their men were being killed in the thousands. Up until this point, Rome had lost hundreds of warships, and its primary focus was to defeat Carthage on land. This strategy did not yield a final victory for Rome because Carthage controlled the sea and could keep sending resources and reinforcements to fight in Sicily. In 249 B.C., Rome suffered an enormous naval defeat at the Battle of Drepana. By the end of 249 B.C., Rome effectively had no navy. For the next five years, there were no major naval engagements, and in 244 B.C. Carthage began to demobilize its navy to save money.

After more than two decades of fighting, Rome finally realized that the only way to win the war was to destroy the Carthaginian navy. Unfortunately, Rome did not have a navy large enough to carry out this ambitious plan nor would the Roman people accept another tax increase to fund such a navy.

The Greek historian, Polybius, writes how Rome was able to raise the funds to rebuild another navy:

> "...there were no funds in the public treasury for this purpose; but yet, owing to the patriotic and generous spirit of the leading citizens, enough was found to carry out the project; as either one, two, or three of them, according to their means, undertook to provide a quinquereme fully equipped on the understanding that they would be repaid if all went well."[63]

How many American billionaires would put their fortunes on the line to save their country in a time of crisis?

The Roman elite personally funded an entire navy to be built because they knew it was the only way to save Rome and win the war. In contrast, the Carthaginian elite had no appetite for staking their fortunes to save their city and their countrymen from defeat. This difference in character would change history. In 242 B.C., Rome's newly built navy quickly defeated Carthage's lethargic naval forces, and Carthage soon surrendered. Carthage was forced to leave Sicily and its surrounding islands and pay approximately 3.4 million ounces of silver to Rome over the next ten years. If Rome had lost, Europe and America would have been very different today, but the Romans won because they had citizens with exceptional character who turned down bribes, rejected peace terms that weakened them in the long term, and put their fortunes on the line to fund a navy so that Rome would be victorious.

Roman society slowly transformed from an honor-based culture to one based on status. This transformation led Romans to compete on the basis of wealth instead of virtue. Instead of pursuing the interests of their nation, Romans began pursuing their own narrow interests. The most glaring example was Julius Caesar, who marched on Rome itself, effectively destroyed the republican tradition, and installed himself as permanent emperor. Did Caesar think about the consequences of making himself dictator? Did he think of the crimes that would follow from this disastrous decision? No, he only thought of his own glory because in the first century B.C. this was the new ethos of Rome: ambition over civic responsibility. Such an ethos is the death of all republics, and if it sounds familiar, it's because it has found a home in the hearts of Americans. The lesson to learn from the fall of the Ancient Roman Republic is that civic responsibility must take precedence over destructive ambition.

5

Historic Civic Failures

There have been countless nations whose people rose up and attempted to dispose of their tyrannical government only to tragically fail in the end. The French Revolution and the 1918 Russian Revolution came tantalizingly close to achieving the ideals that first sparked their occurrence, but in the end they both succumbed to mass killings, dictatorial rule, and unenlightened leadership. There are poignantly palpable lessons Americans can learn and apply to their own civic life.

Lesson 1: The fulfillment of civic duty precedes all progress in society.

Lesson 2: Revolution before enlightenment only replaces one tyranny with another.

Lesson 3: Leaders are mirrors. If we are ignorant, selfish, and shortsighted, don't expect our leaders to be enlightened and selfless.

Lesson 4: Moderate and practical leadership is preferable to utopianism and extremism.

THE FRENCH REVOLUTION

The French Revolution was a direct result of the crimes committed by the French aristocracy against the French commoners combined with the influential enlightenment ideas of Voltaire and Rousseau. The French court at Versailles oppressed the people of France for centuries. They lived lavish lives on the backs of their feudal serfs. The king had godlike power and, of course, misused that power. This misuse of power drove the French people to famine, despair, and revolution. On July 14, 1789, an angry mob attacked the Parisian royal fortress known as the Bastille. The mob killed the governor, freed the prisoners, and commandeered the precious armory. The most momentous event in world history since the fall of the Roman Empire had begun. At the onset, the French people were given stark choices between potential leaders. On one side were moderates, such as Marquis de Lafayette, who advocated for an English-style government run by a parliament elected by the population and overseen by the king. On the other side were the radical republicans, embodied by the Jacobin political club led by Maximillian Robespierre, who advocated for the establishment of a republican government at all costs.

Most modern-day Americans have never heard of Lafayette, but what he represented then and now is of supreme relevance. Lafayette represented practical and moderate government in a time of political upheaval. He was a hero of the American Revolution and close friend of George Washington

111

and Thomas Jefferson. At age nineteen, he traveled from France to America at his own expense and volunteered to fight with the Continental Army without pay. He came from a very wealthy family and could have lived an easy life in France, but his ideals drove him to fight for freedom in America.

Immediately preceding the official start of the revolution, the king had granted numerous concessions to republican leaders, including the establishment of a National Assembly to represent the interests of all French citizens.

On June 27, 1789, Lafayette was elected Vice President of the Assembly. While violent tremors began to pulsate from Paris, Lafayette was a highly respected, influential, and moderating leader who opposed violence. He supported a middle ground between the royalists and the radical republicans.

On July 9, 1789, the French National Assembly began the formal process of drafting a new French constitution and requested submissions for a preamble to the constitution. Lafayette, who had been working with Thomas Jefferson on a draft for the past few months, submitted his final draft to the National Assembly on July 11, and it was adopted as the preamble of the new French Constitution on August 26, 1789.[64]

Lafayette supported a peaceful transition to a constitutional monarchy that upheld the ideals espoused in the Declaration of the Rights of Man and of the Citizen. For all intents and purposes, he wanted to combine the English system of government with the American system.

On July 11, 1789, Lafayette was the only leader who combined universal popularity with a desire for moderate, yet substantial democratic reforms. In short, he was the only one who could lead France away from the abyss. He opposed violence to achieve political ends, and he did not seek to remake human nature—two destructive traits of others vying for power.

Immediately after Lafayette submitted his proposed declaration of rights, the king put in motion events that would incite the French people to take even more dramatic and extreme action. On July 12, news reached Paris that the king had dismissed Jacques Necker and other moderates of the Versailles court and replaced them with hardline royalists. With this move, the people of Paris began to ponder the worst and prepare for a military assault on the city. Thinking that King Louis would send in the military to put down the unrest in Paris, Parisians took preemptive action on Tuesday, July 14. On that fateful day, Parisian mobs overwhelmed the city's armory and decapitated the fortress' governor, Bernard-Rene Launay. Later that day, Jacques de Flesselles, another Parisian leader, was decapitated after refusing to provide weapons to the citizen mobs. Both men's heads were paraded around the city on pikes. A dangerous precedent had been set, one that embraced arbitrary violence against the "enemies of liberty."

Shortly after Parisians occupied the Bastille, Lafayette was named Commander of the Paris National Guard, a role that put Lafayette in the precarious position of maintaining law and order in a city full of violent, starving mobs.

For the next year, Lafayette cast a moderating influence on the French Revolution. One episode in particular exemplifies how Lafayette helped channel the revolutionary energy toward peaceful and productive ends.

According to newspaper accounts, on October 5, 1789,

a mob assembled in Paris' Place de Greve. The mob brought pitchforks, pikes, and even cannons into the public plaza as they protested vehemently against what they believed was a royal plot to drive up bread prices. Lafayette met the crowd and tried to persuade them not to march to Versailles and confront the king, but by 5:00 p.m. that day, the 30,000-person strong mob was out of Lafayette's control and began their march. Lafayette and a contingent of the Paris National Guard shadowed them to the Palace of Versailles. Once the mob arrived, a stalemate ensued as they came up to the palace gates. Lafayette saw the potential for catastrophe and asked permission to speak with the king. Upon entering the king's quarters, Lafayette presented the mob's demands to him. The two most significant demands were that the king entrust the National Guard troops of Paris and Versailles to be his bodyguards and that the royal family relocate their residence to the Tuileries in Paris. Lafayette guaranteed the safety of the royal couple, and they agreed to the terms. In a surprising gesture, Lafayette met Queen Marie Antoinette on the balcony addressing the crowd and bowed to kiss the queen's hand. The crowd erupted in cheers exclaiming, "Vive la reine!"[64] Long live the queen. Lafayette had successfully diffused a situation avoiding mass violence. Other more radical revolutionary leaders would have incited the crowd to violence, but Lafayette mediated a resolution based in civility.

 Unfortunately, Lafayette's leadership was ultimately rejected by the French people in 1791 as they embraced the radical measures advocated by the Jacobin club. This led the French to empower a dictator who would engage in state-sponsored executions.

With Lafayette out of the picture and no moderate leaders left, Robespierre and the radical Jacobins seized power and instituted a Reign of Terror that would kill thousands in the name of liberty. In the spring of 1794, during the most intense time of the Terror, the people of France must have felt intense regret and disappointment in the government they empowered. Nearly five years before, they had cast aside a monarchy that had ruled France for centuries, they had declared the rights of man and pledged to defend liberty. I wonder what they would've seen in the mirror as their countrymen were being slaughtered en masse. The Terror hit its apex when Robespierre turned his back on his childhood friend and fellow republican revolutionary, Camille Desmoulins. Camille was a prominent revolutionary leader who was critical of the Revolutionary government's policy to "kill the enemies of the republic."

As Camille sat in solitary confinement awaiting to be executed, he wrote to his wife, Lucille. His words are immensely touching:

> "You see in my fate an example of the barbarity and ingratitude of men...I carry with me the esteem and regrets of all true Republicans, of all men of virtue and who love liberty. I die at the age of 34 years, but it is marvelous that I have walked for 5 years along the precipices of the Revolution without falling over them, and that I am still living; and I rest my head calmly upon the pillow of my writings, which, too numerous as they may be, all breathe the same philanthropy, the same desire to make my fellow citizens happy and

free, The axe cannot touch them...I have dreamed of a Republic such as all the world would have adored. I could have never believed that men could be so ferocious and so unjust..."[65]

The tragic death of French revolutionary Camille Desmoulins and the deaths of thousands of innocent French citizens during the Reign of Terror would have been avoided had Lafayette and his moderate policies been the guiding light of the revolution. The death warrants may have been signed by Robespierre, but their actions were cheered by the people of France for long enough to commit genocide in the name of freedom. These heinous crimes were ultimately the responsibility of the militant urban poor, the sans-culotte, who were desperate and willing to support terrorism to achieve their political goals and, therefore, unenlightened.

Why did the sans-culotte take a more radical stance and betray any semblance of enlightenment values? Simple. They were not enlightened and therefore unprepared to use power wisely. Why was Robespierre able to murder thousands of French citizens? The French people, namely the sans-culotte, empowered him to do so. They attended the public executions carried out by guillotine and cheered as people's heads were cut off. Did they know why that person was about to be killed? No, their illogic led them to believe that if the accused were innocent, they wouldn't be kneeling under the guillotine. As Robespierre said, "Virtue need no defense." If the French rejected the idea of virtue though terror to achieve political ends, Robespierre would have remained a provincial lawyer, and France may well have known liberty a century sooner.

In the end, the Reign of Terror would only weaken the French first republic and lay the foundation for the French people to demand a Caesar take power and restore order. Caesar came to France in the form of Napoleon Bonaparte. On December 2, 1804, the republic was officially no more when Napoleon coronated himself emperor of the French in Notre Dame Cathedral.[66] What began in 1789 as a revolution based in admirable ideals degenerated into tyranny and back to a dictatorship, which the revolution had originally sought to destroy.

Fortune gave France a chance to avoid the mass killings of the Reign of Terror, the endless Napoleonic Wars, the long-lasting enmities between France and Germany that helped foment two world wars, and the destruction of republican ideals. The mistake the French made in rejecting Lafayette's leadership would take eight decades to correct. France would finally bid adieu to kings, queens, and dictators in 1871 after losing the Franco-Prussian war.

If the French had embodied the ethos of Marquis de Lafayette instead of Maximillian Robespierre, the Reign of Terror would have been avoided, Napoleon would have remained a no-name Corsican, and Europe may well have avoided the horrors of two world wars.

Americans may be tempted by the all-encompassing solutions that extremists offer from the right and the left, but we must remember that the ends do not justify the means. There is nothing wrong with sober, well-reasoned, and rational governance. In the near future, Americans will be tempted by political extremists. The choice the nation makes in that hour will be a fateful one. Let us make that decision wisely.

Peter Magistrale

The Russian Revolution

One hundred twenty-eight years after the beginning of the French Revolution, history would again tragically teach humanity the price of revolution before enlightenment. Under almost identical circumstances, the Russian people sought the end of an entrenched aristocracy and the establishment of democratic rule.

It was February 1917, and World War I was inflicting unprecedented horrors on humanity. Russia was suffering more than any other warring nation. More than 1.5 million Russian soldiers had been killed, and more than four million were wounded. In cities, everyday Russians were contending with the vulture of famine. Czar Nicholas couldn't find an answer to end German superiority in the field, and the Russian people were tired of seeing their countrymen killed.

The fuse was lit on February 23, 1917, in the capital of Petrograd (formerly Saint Petersburg). Mass protests broke out against food rationing and the incompetence of the czarist government. The protests quickly turned violent, and the government lost all control over the city. Soon after the protests broke out, Mikhail Rodzianko, Chairman of the Duma, telegrammed Czar Nicholas.

> "The situation is serious. The capital is in a state of anarchy. The Government is paralyzed. Transport service and the supply of food and fuel have become completely disrupted. General discontent is growing. There is wild shooting in the streets. In places troops are firing at each other...There must be no delay. Any procrastination is tantamount to death."[67]

118

The czar reacted with characteristic misjudgment, believing that the warnings of chaos and revolution were overreactions. Within a week, the Petrograd garrison had mutinied and joined the protesters. Three hundred years of Romanov rule over Russia came to an unceremonious end when Czar Nicholas abdicated the throne in March 1917.

Like the French Revolution, the Russian Revolution began with promise. The provisional government that sprang up after the abdication of Czar Nicholas supported Western-style democratic rights, including equality before the law, freedom of speech, and the right of workers to unionize and strike. The most promising part of the provisional government was their opposition to violent revolution. In many ways, they mirrored the moderates of the French Revolution, specifically Marquis de Lafayette. Unfortunately for millions of Russians, the provisional government made one fatal mistake: it did not end Russian involvement in World War I.

After seeing the czar abdicate the Russian throne and the United States enter the war on the side of the Entente, the German high command devised a plan to rapidly destabilize Russia and force them to sue for peace. The German generals settled on a Russian exile who had made strong public pronouncements supporting the end of Russian involvement in World War I. The man they chose to help end the war on the eastern front was Vladimir Ilyich Ulyanov, more famously known by his revolutionary alias Vladimir Lenin. German general Erich Ludendorff predicted, "Lenin will overthrow the Russian patriots and then I will strangle him—him and all his friends."[68]

At 3:10 p.m. on April 9, 1917, Lenin, a man Winston Churchill would later call the "plague bacillus," departed from Zurich on what the Germans called der Russenzug—the Russian train. The Germans secured safe passage for Lenin from Switzerland, northeast through Germany, further north through Sweden, and finally east and south through Finland, before reaching Finland Station in then Petrograd, Russia. A marching band, playing the violent French revolutionary song and now French national anthem "La Marseillaise," greeted him at 11:00 p.m. on April 16, 1917. The "plague bacillus" had been successfully reintroduced into the Russian body politic.[69]

That night, spotlighted by searchlights, Lenin made a short speech to the revolutionaries gathered at Finland station.

> "Comrade sailors, I greet you without knowing yet whether or not you have been believing in all the promises of the Provisional Government. But I am convinced that when they talk to you sweetly, when they promise you a lot, they are deceiving you and the whole Russian people. The people need peace; the people need bread; the people need land. And they give you war, hunger, no bread—leave the landlords still on the land...We must fight for the social revolution, fight to the end, till the complete victory of the proletariat. Long live the worldwide social revolution!"[70]

Shortly after Lenin arrived in Petrograd, he published the April Theses. The ten directives set out a road map for what would become the October Bolshevik revolution.[71]

120

The most notable directives are summarized below:

1. The end of Russian involvement in a predatory imperialist war
2. All power must be passed to the poorest peasants
3. No support for the Provisional Government...a government of capitalists should cease to be an imperialist government
4. Abolition of the police, the army, and the bureaucracy
5. Confiscation of all landed estates
6. Nationalization of all banks

Robespierre's desire to create a "republic of virtue" in France only led to mass murder. Lenin would follow in Robespierre's footsteps, demagogically calling for a "dictatorship of the proletariat." Lenin promised "land, bread, and peace." The Russian people embraced his revolutionary rhetoric, but like Germany, they would get much more than they bargained for. In July 1917, the Bolsheviks made their next major chess move against the provisional government. Workers and soldiers marched through Petrograd to the Tauride Palace and demanded that the provisional government be replaced by worker soviets.

The demonstrations were not well coordinated, and within a few days they dispersed. Soon after, the republican moderate, Alexander Kerensky, was named prime minister of the provisional government, and the truth of Lenin's close ties with the German government was released to the public. Public opinion began to move against the Bolsheviks, and Lenin was again forced into exile. Later that summer, Kerensky would make a strategic blunder that would allow Lenin and the Bolsheviks to deliver a decisive checkmate.

Commander and Chief of the Russian Army, General Lavr Kornilov, marshalled his army with the intention of descending on Petrograd and exterminating the Bolshevik threat. Kerensky feared Kornilov would establish a military dictatorship and depose him as well. With this threat in mind, Kerensky's provisional government worked with the Petrograd Soviets, dominated by the Bolsheviks, to defend the city against the advancing army. The Soviets collaborated with rail work unions to slow down the army's advance and infiltrated Kornilov's army, convincing soldiers to desert. By the end of August, Kornilov's army was significantly depleted, and he had lost support to attack Petrograd. The battle ended without a shot fired or a life lost, but it laid the foundation for the next battle.

As part of the defense of Petrograd, the provisional government had distributed arms and ammunition to the Bolsheviks in case the city had to be defended by force. Kerensky had played checkers instead of chess. He misjudged the future consequence of arming his enemies, the Bolsheviks, because he was consumed by an attempted right-wing coup by General Kornilov. This misjudgment gave the Bolsheviks the guns to take power. They wasted no time to assert their newfound advantage. On November 7, 1917, the Bolsheviks and the far-left faction of the Socialist Revolutionary Party began to occupy government buildings and key infrastructure points. The next day the Winter Palace was captured along with the entire provisional government cabinet, except Kerensky, who had escaped earlier in the day. Kerensky would fight a civil war against the Bolsheviks until 1922, but the game was lost at this very moment.

Soon after assuming power, Lenin extinguished any hope of Russian democracy. He also kept his word to his German collaborators and the Russian people. On March 3, 1918, Russia signed the harsh terms of the Treaty of Brest-Litovsk. The Russian people leaped out of the frying pan right into the fire—the fire of communism and brutal dictatorship. The Russian people revolted because they wanted to end their involvement in World War I, end the backward Romanov rule, and end the famine that afflicted them. Instead, they empowered a madman who would take joy in starving, killing, and dominating his own people. Lenin was Robespierre reborn in Russian form. After making peace with Germany, Lenin waged a vicious war against Russian peasants. The Russian civil war destroyed Russia's industrial output, impoverished the nation, and spread a nationwide famine. To solve this problem, Lenin came up with a brilliant communist idea: take from those that have and give to those that don't have.

This meant taking the entire crop yield of rural peasants at gunpoint and leaving nothing for them to live on. The result was nothing short of mass genocide. Lenin, with supreme indifference for human life, announced the death sentence of millions. Lenin was the ultimate enemy of the Russian people.

In October 1919, Lenin met with the Russian physiologist Ivan Pavlov. It was "Pavlov's dogs" experiment that interested Lenin. The famous experiment by Pavlov proved that a hungry dog can physiologically associate the ring of a bell with food

123

when the bell is rung before food is given. In other words, after repeated conditioning, the hungry dog would salivate even before food was provided. Lenin told Pavlov:

> "I want the masses of Russia to follow a Communistic pattern of thinking and reacting." Pavlov, taken back by the implications of such a statement asked, "Do you mean that you would like to standardize the population of Russia? Make them all behave in the same way?" Lenin responded in the affirmative, "Exactly. Man can be corrected. Man can be made what we want him to be."[72]

Lenin saw the Russian people as the enemy. The enemy of his dictatorial rule. The enemy of the totalitarian rule of the Communist Party.

After Lenin's policies intentionally led to famine in the Russian countryside, the Russian people must have realized they had allowed a totally insane and inhuman man to take control of their country. Who was responsible for the rise of Lenin and the tragedy of Soviet Russia? The German government and Czar Nicholas all played leading roles in the events that would give birth to the "plague bacillus" that was Vladimir Lenin.

In the final analysis, it was the Russian people, who, by silence or ignorance, empowered a psychopath to destroy them. It was the people who made a valiant attempt to throw aside the aristocratic society of Czarist Russia and replace it with a democratic government that reflected the will of the majority. That ethos of the early revolution was subverted by utopian dreams and demagoguery. If the Russian peasantry understood the nature of power, I hardly believe they would have empowered a dictator. If the Petrograd garrison that defected to the Bolshevik side could've seen the horrors that would be committed in their name, I'm confident they would have sided differently.

Hindsight, of course, is 20/20, but universal laws of human nature were violated due to ignorance, and ignorance was the reason the Russian Revolution failed and millions of Russians lost their lives, dignity, and humanity. We Americans can learn from the failures of the Russian Revolution. The most important lesson we can learn is that power before wisdom is the mother of all tyranny; therefore, knowledge must be our main objective.

The Russian people were sufficiently angry, hungry, and hopeless, but they were not sufficiently wise. They should have known better than to think they could solve their own plight by destroying the wealthy and taking their property. They should have known that when the Bolsheviks promised land for peasants it was raw pandering to acquire power. With knowledge of the French Revolution, the demagogues of classical antiquity, and human nature, the Russian people could have avoided the atrocities of the Soviet Union.

The failures of the French and Russian Revolutions prove that until the people are sufficiently enlightened, revolution is more dangerous than the status quo.

When given the choice between a Cicero and a Caesar, between a Lafayette and a Robespierre, between a Kerensky and a Lenin, the people, more times than not, chose the tyrant. That cataclysmic deficiency in judgment has plagued human

125

history for thousands of years, and at its core is an immense ignorance of the true nature of mankind. Most people the world over are honest, well intentioned, and decent. What they fail to realize is that most who seek power do not share those qualities. Extremism is an excuse to take unprecedented actions that destroy societies but elevate the power of a dictator. People too often fall for the oversimplified solutions, are seduced by pandering, and bribed by handouts. These are lessons to be learned from history. To ignore is to repeat. America is too important to humanity to repeat the civic failures of the Roman Plebs, the French sans-culotte, and the Russian Bolsheviks. To avoid these tragic failures, we must look honestly at our own society, identify our shortcomings, and work to improve ourselves, our communities, and our nation.

6

How We Can Live Up to Our Civic Duty

As Americans, we are leaders of humanity by virtue of being citizens of the most powerful country on earth. Humanity cannot afford another dark age. We must turn this around, not only for Americans, but also for the millions who depend on American moral, economic, and political leadership. We occupy the same position of preeminence that Ancient Rome held in antiquity. We occupy this position not because of our own doing but because of the genius of the men who crafted our constitution and the bravery of the soldiers who fought to keep us free from tyranny. We cannot rest on the achievements of our forefathers and the sacrifices of past generations. We must raise our quality as citizens and make equal, if not greater, contributions to America than previous generations. The greatest contribution we can make is to simply commit to lifelong self-improvement. Our improvement as individuals will undoubtedly permeate into our politics, economy, and culture.

Petrarca

The fall of Rome led to an 800 year decline in Western civilization. The flame of knowledge, progress, and human achievement was abruptly extinguished. Man succumbed to superstition, lost critical knowledge, and embraced ignorance.

This darkness did not lift until the people of Europe began to rekindle their interest in the achievements, knowledge, and ideas of Ancient Greece and Rome. The man credited for starting the fire that would lead to the European Renaissance and end the Dark Ages was Francesco Petrarca. Petrarca was an Italian poet and classical scholar who, at the time, had an uncommon interest in ancient Rome. This interest was born out of a desire to escape the backwardness of his own time. He regarded the Middle Ages as an epoch of ignorance where people were entranced by the divine at the expense of human welfare. Glory could be restored if man put his talents and abilities into the service of discovering knowledge and using that knowledge to solve human problems. This philosophy became known as humanism, and its focus was on humanity—our potential, our abilities, and our achievements. This sounds like a common sense way to approach human problems, but in the Dark Ages, all confidence in mankind was lost because the major stabilizing power, Rome, was destroyed and replaced by the stifling ideology of Judeo-Christianity. Petrarca was a Catholic man, but he broke from tradition by professing his confidence in humanity's ability to solve its own problems. That simple idea, grounded in humble ambition, would come to define Renaissance humanism and transform European society at a turning point in history.

Cicero

Petrarca's pursuit of ancient knowledge led him to discover previously unknown works written by the famous Roman statesman, Cicero.

Of all of Cicero's works, none was more responsible in igniting the Renaissance than *On Duties*.

In this published work, intended to educate his son Brutus on the duties he faced as a Roman citizen, Cicero lucidly offers counsel not only for his son but also for posterity.[73]

1. Civic obligation to society is a fundamental duty as a citizen

Without a sense of civic duty, society is immediately weakened and inevitably destroyed. Since human beings achieve more collectively in groups rather than as atomized individuals, it follows that humanity at large is weakened when a sense of civic duty is absent. To be clear, civic duty does not mean blind obedience to the prevailing government but rather a constant long term 30,000 foot perspective on the issues facing the community you live in and the nation you call home. It requires an enlightened self-interest that allows you to see the whole picture, not just the immediate impact on your own interests. Above all else, civic duty means defending the ideals and institutions that preserve freedom, harshly punishing those who attempt to commit crimes in pursuit of political goals, and repelling all who attempt to gain power through demagoguery. That is the baseline duty of each American citizen, but if we seek to contribute to America's continued greatness, we must do much more than that. We must look at our fellow citizens not as strangers but as comrades born in the most important time in human history, in the most important country. We must see in each other the potential for greatness and lift each other up. We must see not only our importance to our family but also our importance to our community, our country, and humanity at large. What we contribute individually, here and now, can transform human civilization for time immemorial. It all begins with a sense of civic duty that we have to the United States and each other.

2. Humans alone are unique in their capacity for reason and should use this divine gift to live virtuous lives

We cannot afford to go through life sleepwalking. We have a unique ability to reason, and although not perfect, it offers far greater human benefits than living like a beast enslaved to sensual pleasures, the irrationality of ignorance, and the destruction fear inflicts. Furthermore, we must use reason to live virtuously. To use reason in any other way and live in any other way is a dishonor. The ability to think rationally is what separates mankind from beast. The ability to think is what gives human beings the power to transform themselves. The ability to transform is only activated when we think rationally and act accordingly.

3. Selling your time for money is a pledge of your slavery

To be a dignified citizen capable of fulfilling our civic duty, we cannot sell ourselves into bondage. To accept an indefinite dependence on selling your time for money just to live is an affront to life itself. It implicitly sends the message that you have nothing better to do than have someone else order you around and control your time. How can one be an autonomous citizen if one is not financially independent? It's also an affront because each of us has talents and unique contributions we can make to the world, and how can those priceless contributions be made if we are indefinitely enslaved to a job? The position of an employee is an efficient tool for social engineering. An employee is a slave. A slave does not control their time or their work. A slave must do what he's told or risk putting himself and his family in material danger from not having food or shelter. How can one be a competent citizen if one has not secured their most basic needs first?

We should all be striving for some level of financial independence that allows us to better live according to our will and conscience.

4. We must always guard against the feebleness and idleness that excessive luxury promotes

Wealth, if secured through legal industry and honest dealings, is evidence of the value we provide to society, but wealth, like power, can easily corrupt us. If we accumulate wealth but then lose our industriousness and the virtues that informed our wealth creation, then what purpose does wealth serve? We must understand that wealth is a means to an end, never an end of itself.

5. Those who make pleasure their end soon lose their dignity

The purpose of life is not the perpetual pursuit of sensual pleasures, and those who follow that road are sure to lose a critical aspect of their humanity. Pleasure is a seductive mistress

> *Those who encounter truth in horror will retreat into the comfort of delusion.*
>
> Peter Magistrale

that inserts a cool blade slowly into your soul. Pleasure is the enemy of virtue and foreign to achievement. Let us examine why pleasure cannot guide our character. To achieve anything worthwhile, we must endure resistance and pain. Pain is part of the process of becoming. Common sense tells us that pain is the opposite of pleasure. Therefore, if pleasure is our mistress, we will avoid pain, but that means we will forgo opportunities for growth, achievement, and honor.

There are many things in life that require us to endure pain to become better human beings. The most fundamental example is truth. If we are not willing to pursue the truth wherever it may lead, we are cowards, but to have the courage to pursue the truth, we must be willing to endure temporary pain. Why does the truth cause pain? The truth destroys belief systems, worldviews, and, most of all, illusions that make us feel good. By destroying psychological support columns, they inflict pain on our psyche as we realize our profound ignorance. We realize we were lied to, that we know nothing, and that we must endeavor to build a new worldview based on the truth. The unfortunate soul who seeks pleasure will encounter the truth in horror and retreat into the comfort of their delusions. This a corruption of our character, a negation of our rational potential, and destructive to humanity at large.

We see this retreat from truth in personal relationships when people refuse to believe their partner is cheating on them or engaging in criminal activity. We see it when people are too blinded by misplaced patriotism to see the crimes of their leaders. We see it when people work at jobs they hate but never turn their hatred into motivation to build a new life because they are brainwashed

132

by the prevailing culture. There's nothing wrong with enjoying pleasure, but when it becomes the standard that guides our character, it thoroughly corrupts us.

6. Nothing can be expedient that is not morally right

This principle requires us to see the long term consequences of our actions. We must be willing to measure not only the consequences of tomorrow but also the consequences that may arise many years in the future from our immoral decisions today.

These ideas, espoused by Cicero, ignited the Renaissance because they put forward a revolutionary value system for people to model their lives around—a value system that appealed to them because it yielded far greater benefits than the value system imposed on them by the backwardness of the Dark Ages.

Civic humanism and an emphasis on living a virtuous life are revolutionary because the corrupt power structure, whether it be the Catholic Church of Medieval Europe or the plutocracy of modern times, can only exist if the citizenry is corrupt.

Cicero's ideas, more perennial than original, nonetheless are a blueprint to enlighten a corrupt citizenry. The enlightenment of each citizen must be the foremost preoccupation of all who seek the advancement of mankind. Those who seek domination over humanity depend on ignorance, apathy, hopelessness, vanity, and petty distractions to exert their illegitimate power. Caesar destroyed the Roman Republic because the Roman people had lost their virtue as citizens.

It is clear to see why Cicero's ideas on civic virtue and humanism inspired a rebirth within medieval Europe. He inspired people to rethink their value system, their role in the world, and how they should live. Cicero helped lift men from their knees and see that human beings can achieve marvelously, can solve unimaginable problems, and maintain their dignity while living virtuously. The difference between focusing on personal responsibility and deferring responsibility to divine power creates an extraordinary chasm between human beings and societies. Petrarca was a messenger that transferred this powerful message from Classical Rome to Medieval Europe and helped put humanity on the path to progress.

America has reaped significant rewards as a result of the achievements of a small group of Americans. To address our nation's systemic political, social, and cultural problems, we all must take personal responsibility for causing the current state of affairs and then take direct action to become more informed, make evidence based decisions, and live with purpose. We must embrace our duties as American citizens not only to improve our nation, but also to ensure the most powerful country on Earth is leading the world in solving the most pressing problems of our time.

The consequences of too many Americans living without a sense of civic duty and without a sense of purpose are catastrophic to our nation's future.

José Ortega y Gasset

The largely unknown but nonetheless prescient twentieth century Spanish philosopher, José Ortega y Gasset, observed the difference between people who put duties on themselves and strive toward excellence and people who reject that value system.

He wrote in his 1929 book, *Revolt of the Masses*:

"The most radical division that it is possible to make of humanity is that which splits it into two classes of creatures: those who make great demands on themselves, piling up difficulties and duties; and those who demand nothing special of themselves, but for whom to live is to be every moment what they already are, without imposing on themselves any effort towards perfection, mere buoys that float on the waves."[74]

The fundamental difference between someone who pursues achievement as opposed to luxury and ease is in their respective value systems. The person who pursues achievement seeks out the challenges that, when overcome, lead them closer to their ultimate goal. They see pain as temporary and indispensable on the road to greatness. The value that guides them is perpetual personal improvement. This decision leads to a nearly different species of human beings. On the other end of the spectrum is someone who avoids pain, challenges, and resistance at all costs. This quickly leads to atrophy, everlasting ignorance, and personal stagnation. Can a nation of hedonistic pleasure seeking citizens be enlightened? Never. Can a nation of comfort-seeking citizens ever stand up to the crimes of their leaders? They would be too weak to do anything but watch football on Sunday.

Why should we care how other people live their lives? Shouldn't we live and let live? No, that is a selfish and misguided approach. People who don't care about how their fellow citizens live also don't care about the community and nation they live in. They fail to realize that the actions or inactions of their fellow citizens have a significant impact on them and the nation they live in.

Obviously, we shouldn't use compulsion to force people to live a certain way, but we should persistently insist that they reject the values that weaken them and enslave them to the darkness that surrounds them. How flawed is mankind. Someone who does not seek personal improvement either rejects the value of their life or implicitly says they're perfect. Who, with dignity, can honestly attest to either statement? Our focus shouldn't be on our flaws but on our potential to transform and to become a person much greater than the one who stares at us in the mirror.

The great tragedy of life is dying before you have seen the full extent of your skills, talents, and fortitude. The great crime committed by humanity is dying before leaving an indestructible gift for their fellow citizens. We should endeavor to always contribute more to our communities, society, and country than we've taken. We live unfinished lives when we live the unexamined life. Only someone who failed to examine their life could erect comfort or pleasure atop their value system. Only someone profoundly ignorant of their mortality could waste time on the temporal and selfish. Strength, whether physical or mental, comes from persistence in the face of resistance.

Another key point to be aware of is that who you become in the process of pursuing a great endeavor or living up to a great ideal is more important than achieving your immediate goal. Even if the goal you sought eludes you, in the end you are stronger and more capable for the next challenge. To embrace this mentality, we must delay gratification for long periods of time. This is diametrically opposed to the ethos that drives our economy, which dictates we must consume today to be comfortable, sexier, youthful, or whatever some hollow vessel on Madison Avenue is trying to sell. The consumer culture that has been brainwashed into Americans sacrifices their long term interests for their short-term appetites. This culture was created by the wealthy to ensure they had a constant market for their goods. We are all bombarded by this programming, and if we seek greatness, we must deprogram ourselves of this self-destructive psychological infection. The only way to take a scalpel to the cultural brainwashing inculcated in us is to live the examined life. If you examine your beliefs, actions, and values, you will see that you hold beliefs and take actions that go against who you truly want to become. If you never examine yourself, you will live according to the psychological programming of the prevailing culture. That programming serves a purpose near and dear to the elite. They want people to make money and then spend it all on products the elite sell so that they then have to be wage slaves their whole lives. They want people on the earn, spend, work, and repeat cycle because such people don't have time to challenge the elite in the arena that matters most: politics. It also simultaneously weakens their enemy (the masses) economically, culturally, and politically, making them easier to control and manipulate.

The myths of our culture must be discarded. The lies we've been told must be eviscerated. The truth must be pursued no matter where it leads and no matter how bad it makes us feel in the moment. We must guide our thinking, our values, and our actions on reality. Illusions only serve those that disseminate illusions. Who needs illusions the most? The powerful, and why do they need illusions? It makes life easier for them to act without accountability and pursue their own interests as opposed to the interests of their fellow citizens. The powerful invest heavily in the illusions that pervade American society, and the masses are heavily invested in those illusions because it provides a sense of short-term comfort. If comfort is what you seek, you will have no problem finding the illusions that suit your psychological needs. The political and cultural illusions infect the soul of America. It need not be this way forever. It all begins with each individual's decision to pursue great deeds, to pursue the truth, and to reject the siren's call of comfort and ease. To be a more enlightened nation, we need to live in a more enlightened manner, and the first step is adopting an enlightened value system and acting consistently with that value system.

Ortega later adds:

> "For me, then, nobility is synonymous with a life of effort, ever set on excelling oneself, in passing beyond what one is to what one sets up as a duty and an obligation. In this way the noble life stands opposed to the common or inert life, which reclines statically upon itself, condemned to perpetual immobility, unless an external force compels it to come out of itself. Hence we apply the term mass to this kind of man—not so much because of his multitude as because of his inertia."

Whether one believes they can transform or not is of supreme importance to our society. Personal and professional transformation can only occur if the individual believes they are capable of changing their habits, actions, and thoughts. This is especially important when public school and propaganda conspire to make everyone equally mediocre and dull. To create a great goal for oneself and then pursue it demands that you unlearn all of the programming our culture has imprinted on you. Ortega makes a brilliant observation:

> "As one advances in life, one realizes more and more that the majority of men—and of women—are incapable of any other effort than that strictly imposed on them as a reaction to external compulsion. And for that reason, the few individuals we have come across who are capable of a spontaneous and joyous effort stand out isolated, monumentalized, so to speak, in our experience. These are the select men, the nobles, the only ones who are active and not merely reactive, for whom life is a perpetual striving, an incessant course of training."

How many of us live under the threat of compulsion? We go to school and learn things that are irrelevant. We go to work and do pointless work because we need money to live. Our time is robbed from us, and by the end of the night, we have no energy to pursue things we truly feel passionate about. Once we do this for long enough, we give up on pursuing our dreams and let compulsion rule us.

139

"Take stock of those around you and you will see them wandering about lost through life, like sleep-walkers in the midst of their good or evil fortune, without the slightest suspicion of what is happening to them. You will hear them talk in precise terms about themselves and their surroundings, which would seem to point to them having ideas on the matter. But start to analyze those ideas and you will find they hardly reflect in any way the reality to which they appear to refer, and if you go deeper you will discover there is not even an attempt to adjust the ideas to this reality. Quite the contrary: through these notions the individual is trying to cut off any personal vision of reality, of his own very life."

Why are so many of us lost? We are lost because we don't think about how we live our lives. We do the unforgivable and live unexamined lives. By doing so, our lives are guided by the vicissitudes of life. We find ourselves when we seek to understand the world, our place in it, and our purpose. Purpose gives us the clarity and strength to know where we are going in life and gives meaning to the pain and challenges we encounter. Too many of us don't want to know the truth because we can't control it, but we can control the lies we make up in our heads. Those lies create illusions that justify our inaction, justify our ignorance, and justify us not pursuing, in the end, what is most important. This process of self-deception harms society just as much as the individual. Society is degraded because the individual does not pursue their purpose, does not self-actualize, and consequently does not make a meaningfully positive impact on the world around them. We should strive to see the best in our fellow citizens brought forward, and we should strive to bring out the best in ourselves. This is the best antidote to all the ills of humanity. The answers to our problems are in the collective human race. If only we could uncover the riches in each of us, what would the world look like then?

> "As they say in the United States: "...to be different is to be indecent. The mass crushes beneath it everything that is different, everything that is excellent, individual, qualified and select. Anybody who is not like everybody, who does not think like everybody, runs the risk of being eliminated."

"Know the truth and it will make you odd"; Eudora Welty

People who diverge from mainstream culture are naturally ostracized because they make people question themselves. The minimalist indicts the consumerist. The freethinker indicts the conformist. Those who seek freedom have contempt for hedonists. People are so invested in the culture they've been programmed to follow that they viciously defend their prison. The consumerist is a slave to soulless materialism. The conformist is controlled by the opinions of others. The pleasure lover is a slave to his five senses. All three archetypes are not free. It would be in everyone's self-interest to value material goods less, think more, and seek freedom. I doubt many people would disagree with that statement, but yet look at the culture we live in. People may agree in theory that consumerism, conformism, and hedonism are contrary to human well being, but rarely will they acknowledge their participation and, even rarer, will they change their behavior. This is because Americans are willing to pay any price to be accepted by the group and avoid being ostracized.

Herein lies a fundamental human need: the need to be socially accepted within a valued group, but also a fundamental flaw because if the group is corrupt, unenlightened, and unjust, then you're aligning your guiding values with the values of fools. This begs the question: Why do people, more times than not, lack the courage to go against society and follow their conscience? It all comes down to the psychology of self-worth and survival.

To many, social isolation means nothing less than death. The reptilian brain sees the potential for social isolation as a dystopian future for the self that must be averted at all costs. "No price is too high to avoid social isolation"; these poor souls are commanded by their own fears. While social isolation is a terrible cost to pay for following your conscience, it must be weighed against the tyrannical fee that an unenlightened crowd may charge for admission into their party of fools.

There is a keen difference between professed values and the values people actually live by. What are the values expressed more than any other in American society? Instant gratification, selfishness, and willful ignorance.

This type of thinking has preceded many genocides, numerous wars, and the fall of civilizations. From the Roman Empire to Hitler, Stalin, and Mao, history shows us that groupthink is absolute poison to human society, but it is paramount for centralized control over the minds of the masses.

It may sound strange and unrealistic that America could suffer a similar fall from grace, but America is only as good as its citizens, and its citizens are only as good as the value system they live by. America will fall if Americans do not rise. To rise, we, Americans, must live in a way that values truth, excellence, and noble purpose.

PLATO

To understand how Americans perceive reality, one is well served to read the timeless thoughts of the Ancient Greek philosopher, Plato.

Written nearly 2,500 years ago, *The Republic* by Plato outlined how an ideal city could be built. Using his mentor Socrates as the teacher and an Athenian citizen named Glaucon as the student, Plato describes the famous Allegory of the Cave in Book 7 of *The Republic*.

> "Imagine human beings living in an underground, cave like dwelling, with an entrance a long way up, which is both open to the light and as wide as the cave itself. They've been there since childhood, fixed in the same place, with their necks and legs fettered, able to see only in front of them, because their bonds prevent them from turning their heads around. Light is provided by a fire burning far above and behind them. Also, behind them, but on higher ground, there is a path stretching between them and the fire. Imagine that along this path a low wall has been built, like the screen in front of puppeteers above which they show their puppets..."[75]

This is akin to the brainwashing and propaganda that are disseminated through the popular culture. The purpose of this propaganda is to have each citizen perceive the world in a manner that is acceptable to those in power. Divergent ideas and worldviews must be the exception, not the rule; otherwise, the illusions of the cave will be exposed, and those in power will be thrown from their high places. It cannot be stressed enough how important illusions are to the maintenance of the current corrupt order.

> "Then also imagine that there are people along the wall, carrying all kinds of artifacts that project above it—statues of people and other animals, made out of stone, wood, and every material. And, as you'd expect, some of the carriers are talking, and some are silent... And what if their prison also had an echo from the wall facing them? Don't you think they'd believe that the shadows passing in front of them were talking whenever one of the carriers passing along the wall was doing so?"

These shadows in the modern day would be exemplified by fans fetishizing professional sports, obsessing over celebrities, and acting like mindless consumers. The shadows are anything that distracts you from pursuing your purpose. They are distractions to keep people occupied enough to not pursue the truth. We are these cave dwellers Plato described so many years ago.

> "Then the prisoners would in every way believe that the truth is nothing other than the shadows of those artifacts. Consider, then, what being released from their

We live in the shadows of the material world and our material beings do not see the true reality that we are spiritual beings having a material/human experience.

We The People Are The Problem

bonds and cured of their ignorance would naturally be like if something like this came to pass...What do you think he'd say, if we told him that what he'd seen before was inconsequential?...I suppose, then, that he'd need time to get adjusted before he could see things in the world above...Finally, I suppose, he'd be able to see the sun, not images of it in water or some alien place, but the sun itself...At this point he would infer and conclude that the sun provides the seasons and the years, governs everything in the visible world, and is in some way the cause of all the things that he used to see."

the spirit is real and the material world is just a shadow of the spiritual source

—of all that exists. Our true spiritual

Most people mistake effect for cause because their ignorance is so profound. Correcting this error in reasoning is life changing.

beings pass through the material world like

"What about when he reminds himself of his first dwelling place, his fellow prisoners, what passed for wisdom there? Don't you think that he'd count himself happy for the change and pity the others? And if there had been any honors, praises, or prizes among them for the one who was sharpest at identifying the shadows as they passed by...do you think that our man would desire these rewards or envy those among the prisoners who were honored and held power? Instead, wouldn't he rather, like Achilles, be a serf on Earth than a king in the underworld? Consider this too. If this man went down into the cave again and sat down in his same seat, wouldn't his eyes, coming suddenly out of the sun like that, be filled with darkness?...And before his eyes

a shadow that moves blatantly fleetingly across the around and disappears from sight but

remains eternally present in the universal field of consciousness.

MZ: 12-1-20

> had recovered and the adjustment would not be quick, while his vision was still dim, if he had to compete again with the perpetual prisoners in recognizing the shadows, wouldn't he invite ridicule?"

I played baseball at the Division I collegiate level, but once I began to realize the nature of the world and my own ignorance, following sports and religiously watching my favorite teams seemed like a colossal waste of time. The average baseball fan now knows far more than I do about the shadows because once you turn your essence around toward pursuing excellence, truth, and wisdom, everything else seems like a waste of time. Following sports teams and celebrities does not change your life, and it does not get you closer to your ultimate goal. It's a form of entertainment that amounts to nothing but a distraction. Too many of us are seduced by the shadows of our society that we lose sight of true value.

> "Wouldn't it be said of him that he'd returned from his upward journey with his eyesight ruined and that it isn't worthwhile even to try to travel upward? And, as for anyone who tried to free them and lead them upward, if they could somehow get their hands on him, wouldn't they kill him?"

Plato's view of the cave of ignorance and how truth seekers risk being killed was informed by the fact that his mentor, Socrates, was put to death by a jury of five hundred fellow Athenian citizens for corrupting the youth. Socrates did nothing more than promote a questioning nature and a pursuit of intellectual truth. To every government that has ever existed, this type of nature makes committing crimes and carrying out deceitful machinations much harder.

This allegory is a perfect metaphor for the world we live in. It explains how so many of us are not free, yet take no action to pursue our dreams and deepest desires. The phenomenon is purely psychological and rooted in fear. The fear of the unknown and unfamiliar. The fear of rebuilding your life. The fear of a great battle. The fear that your life is being wasted. These thoughts keep people, especially Americans, imprisoned in a psychological cave of ignorance. You must be willing to follow reason and evidence wherever it leads you. If you reject these loyal stewards, you will be betrayed by their counterparts, namely illusions.

Plato understood that the five senses could be deceived, and that without the pursuit of truth, mankind would live in a perpetual cave of ignorance. More disturbing than the cave itself is the propensity of the cave dwellers to prefer ignorance to truth and to become happy with their ignominious abode. With the advent of public school, television, and the Internet, it has never been easier for the powerful to manipulate what the common person perceives as reality.

Before the nineteenth century, compulsory public school never existed, before the twentieth century, the television did not exist, and before the twenty first century, the Internet, as we know it, did not exist. Plato would've seen these "advancements" as important tools used by social engineers to shape opinions, dull minds, and make people safe and predictable for

147

[Handwritten annotation at top: Fox News, Hannity & the likes is about keeping people in ignorance so that the powerful elite can control and manipulate them to their own advantage]

society's real rulers. No one can manipulate you unless you disregard the pursuit of knowing what is true about yourself and the world around you. For many, the spark of truth is never ignited because their personality is more in tune with the shallow shadows of life, others are extinguished by the indoctrination of their teachers, and the lucky few who are able to objectively see the illusions of their culture are shunned and ostracized. Too many of us are hopelessly invested in the illusions that keep us imprisoned— "America is a democracy", "Public school is good for my children," "I can't quit my soul destroying job," "The government can't keep secrets," "Experts can be trusted", the plethora of illusions seems endless. What is not endless is our time on this planet, and what a tragedy it is to waste this precious time living in a state of ignorance that degrades our mind, body, and soul.

Most importantly, Plato's Allegory of the Cave highlights a fundamental human truth that ignorance is our only true enemy, and the only way to combat this deceitful traitor of the human spirit is to pursue knowledge and wisdom. Furthermore, Plato is correct, even 2,500 years later, that most people turn their back on the truth and are conquered by deception and lies. Understanding Plato's views on ignorance has had an extraordinarily powerfully positive influence on my life, and that wisdom is priceless for a nation struggling with ignorance and truth.

DEATH AS MOTIVATION

When we think of possible motivation to change ourselves and pursue difficult goals, rarely do we think that death can motivate us, but ironically it may be the best motivator for change.

We The People Are The Problem

How we handle the existential crisis that occurs when we become keenly aware of our mortality is of significant importance to our self-actualization. Some people respond to this crisis nihilistically proclaiming, "What's the point of living if I'm going to die?" They view death as an invalidation of any purpose to life. Where there is no purpose, you are sure to find less than optimal living. Life is what we make it, so why not use death to the advantage of our temporal vitality? The two ways to strategically use death to our advantage are to view death as a relentless motivator to embrace the importance of life and as a validation of the gift of life.

How can the infinite void of death be in any way motivational? Being keenly aware of our mortality should be a reminder that we have no time to waste, and we have nothing to lose. Embodying these truths makes us powerful beings. When we recognize that our time on this planet is just a speck of time in the grand scheme of the universe, we hold our lives to the highest standards and assign the highest values. We no longer accept anything that wastes our time or that does not bring long term and sustainable value to us. Instead of being distracted with whatever spectacle is being force fed to us through the media, we develop a laser focus that seeks out likeminded people and the knowledge to fulfill our purpose and potential. We seek to replicate the intelligence of the universe in our own lives. What is it about beauty in the universe that elicits positive thoughts in human beings? It is the perfection, the harmony, the congruency, the balance, the strength, and the symmetry of what we perceive. If we utilize these characteristics that make up beauty in the universe and we combine them with our transformative character, we can alchemize ourselves from base metal into universal diamond.

To exemplify this entire process, let's analyze one of the most astonishing achievements of intelligent life as we know it—the human body. Our biology is nothing short than the work of hyperintelligence. We have ten major systems in our body all working synergistically and efficiently to achieve one purpose—maintaining our vitality. These systems are the skeletal, muscular, cardiovascular, digestive, immune, nervous, urinary, reproductive, endocrine, and respiratory. Each of these systems is a complex configuration of processes that are guided by our DNA. This intelligence is built on an astounding atomic purpose.

Consider this: All ten major biological systems are working toward one purpose, but when we become aware that these systems are made of trillions of cells, then we realize that trillions of individual cells are working day in and day out to ensure we stay alive. That is the quintessence of purpose. We can apply this line of thinking toward our own lives to fulfill our potential. We all have rather complicated lives with many moving parts affecting our emotional, psychological, economic, and social well being. If we strive to replicate the consistency and singularity of purpose that exists in our bodies and apply it to our own lives, then we are very likely to create masterpieces for which our purpose is focused on. All of this is the end result of looking death in the face and saying, "You may get me one day, but until that day you will be part of my motivation for greatness that will fuel my ascent to the heavens."

If there is no material death then there is an infinite supply of time in the material world and thus life time becomes of little value. That is why we do not

We The People Are The Problem

Another way to transcend the paralyzing fear of death is recognizing a strange truth. Although we may intuitively think that death is the antithesis of life, is this truly the case? We must ponder what value life would have if there was no death. Think for a minute how nihilistic life would be without death. Life is valued so greatly for obvious reasons. The living don't have a lot of time on this planet, and that motivates us to pursue our progress and potential so that each successive generation is better off than we are. How would human society function if life were infinite? First, life would lose all value immediately. What would be the motivation for living well? People would likely procrastinate in perpetuity, feeding each other's misery because of an absence of purpose and consequences. In short, the absence of death would destroy human society because of its negation for what makes us human. Strangely enough, our temporal existence is our greatest asset. It demands a sense of urgency, it presents consequences for not living up to our full potential, and it pushes us to place the highest value on our lives. All of these aid in our ascent to our own personal omega point. It is another ingenious way that the universe affirms life.

The way we frame death can either cripple us or catapult us. If you are to fulfill your potential as an individual and if we are to fulfill our potential as a species, we must view death not as something that leads us toward nihilism but an event with 100 percent certainty to occur at the end of our lives that gives our lives extraordinary value and purpose. Our mortality does not betray us. It invigorates us to live well so that we can die well. Death is the universe's way of motivating the living. Do not let death be a source of paralysis. Rather, use it to your own

remember our own finite lives. If we did, then life would appear to either value and the sense of urgency to achieve our goals before

advantage as a source of personal power to keep you moving up the steepest of life's slippery slopes.

An age-old question that has haunted Man since the beginning of time is what is the purpose of my life? I wasn't alive for billions of years, and miraculously here I am, and on a cosmic scale, I will be gone in a blink of an eye. What do I do with these circumstances? Is there any real meaning to life, or are we a cosmic malfunction in the grand sea of the universe? If there is a central purpose to life, then what, in God's name, is that purpose? These are the types of questions that men and women have asked ever since advanced Man could perceive his condition. The current generation of humanity has access to the wisdom of thousands of years of human contributions to these questions. We do not have all the answers, but we are better equipped than any other generation of mankind to shed light on these existential questions.

The first beautiful piece of ancient wisdom that is timeless and always relevant for Man's utilization is that Man becomes what he thinks about. The universe does not equip us with directions on how to live life. There is no explicit communication from a divine source that humanity was created for a specific purpose. We must transcend what can be perceived as the infinite abyss of Man's purposeless condition by creating our own life purpose. There is no universal purpose of life as far as we can perceive. We must give ourselves that purpose. How do we know the reason we were put on this planet? We pay attention to the people, ideas, and forces that create tremendous emotional accord in us. Life is meant to be lived with fiery passion. To find your purpose, you must pay attention to what ignites within you the passion to transcend your weaknesses, fears, and insecurities. That which inspires and triggers a powerful soul response is your divine purpose.

What is a soul response? It is an overwhelming surge in emotion ignited by a thought, an idea, a vision that is involuntary and emanates from deep within you. The surge in emotion can be so overwhelming that it triggers crying. Not the crying of sadness or depression, but the crying caused by the release of your life purpose from your subconscious to your conscious. The surge electrifies your chest and alters your life irreparably. You literally become a new person. New neurons have formed in your mind by new thoughts and will lead to new action and change the trajectory of your life. Knowing your life purpose makes you a force to be reckoned with. This newfound power is necessary for the path to fulfilling your potential.

Malcolm X

The power of purpose allows us to create a new value system that is nothing short of a personal revolution of the mind. This revolution triggers the actions, beliefs, and thoughts that manifest our greatness. Let's look at a real life example of this revolutionary and powerful transformation to better understand how we can find our purpose and achieve our greatness. Malcolm Little was born in 1925 in a small town in Nebraska. At the age of six, his father was murdered by white supremacists, and by the age of ten, his mother had suffered an emotional breakdown and was admitted to a mental institution. The young Little was separated from his brothers and sisters and sent to an orphanage home.

Peter Magistrale

At the age of twenty one, he was arrested for burglary. He was a young black man with no college education, no family, and no purpose. During his time in prison, Mr. Little began to rebuild himself by becoming an autodidact. He focused his attention on the philosophy of Islam, and at the age of twenty seven, he was reborn as Malcolm X. A seemingly petty criminal in a deeply racist society with no education became one of the leaders of the Civil Rights Movement that advanced the human rights of African Americans.

How could this be possible? Malcolm Little found his life purpose, and this created a total revolution that transformed Malcolm Little, the petty criminal, into Malcolm X, the eloquent and thought provoking orator who was a voice for those without one. Far from being a perfect human being, Malcolm X exemplifies the inherit ability we all have to transform our lives and contribute to the advancement of mankind. He is not an inspiration to just people of color. He is an inspiration to all people. Malcolm X's life shows us the power of purpose, the capability to transform, and our ability to will our enlightened rebirth.

The same applies to our collective society. We must not only find our personal purpose. We must also find our society's purpose. By creating a purpose for society, we ensure that we have laser focus and always move forward with advancing our civilization. Decisions become much easier to make, leaders become much easier to identify, and problems become much easier to solve. By having an explicit, dynamic, and inspiring purpose, people are held together in mutual solidarity for one another, and human life is enriched.

What is the purpose of the USA? What values underlie this purpose?

Conclusion

In 1940 the German-American scholar, Peter Viereck, wrote:

> "Someday the same Germans, now cheering Hitler's strut into Paris, will say to their American friends and to their brave German anti-Nazi friends: "We did not know what went on, we did not know" and when that day of know-nothing comes, there will be laughter in hell.[76]

America occupies a position of enormous importance in the world. We have the strongest military, the largest economy, and vast influence. We have the power to solve humanity's greatest problems, but also the power to light the world on fire. Whether America serves enlightened or destructive ends will ultimately rest with the American people.

A revolution is needed, not in human nature, but in human values and human decision making. Until we become more enlightened citizens, our leaders will reflect our debasement and our laws will reflect our ignorance.

No political party, media outlet, or fringe activist holds primary responsibility for America's decline. We the People are the problem, and if you have had enough of being the problem, then embrace your civic duty. Find a problem you're passionate about and contribute to the solution.

Big Brothers Big Sisters has a waiting list of thousands of youth who do not have a mentor because not enough people volunteer. Don't riot or loot – volunteer! No young person who desperately needs a mentor should be implicitly told no one wants to help them. There are countless ways to have a positive effect on your community, and if you could change the life of even just one person, wouldn't that be worth it?

What is at stake is not just America's future, but the future of humanity. Americans are stewards of democracy, individual rights, and human excellence.

Will you live up to your civic duty? When the next demagogue arrives promising paradise, will you fall for the pandering? When you are given the choice between a Cicero and a Caesar, I hope Cicero is your choice.

If you found this book to be intellectually stimulating the best way to show support is to leave a review. If you want to get in touch with me to discuss ideas mentioned in the book or discuss American society in general, I can be reached at petermagistraleauthor@gmail.com.

Works Cited

1. Caldwell, Taylor. *A Pillar of Iron: A Novel of Ancient Rome*. United States: Open Road Media, 2017.
2. Breitman, Kendall. "Poll: Americans' Sense of Civic Duty Wanes." POLITICO, December 29, 2014. https://www.politico.com/story/2014/12/americans-civic-duty-poll-113853.
3. Gallup. "Congress and the Public." Gallup.com. Gallup, February 13, 2020. https://news.gallup.com/poll/1600/congress-public.aspx.
4. Open Secrets. "Reelection Rates Over the Years." OpenSecrets.org. https://www.opensecrets.org/overview/reelect.php.
5. Wilson, Woodrow. "The Meaning of a Liberal Education." *High School Teachers Association of New York* 3 (1909).
6. Inglis, Alexander James. *The Principles of Secondary Education*. New York: The MACMILLAN COMPANY, 1922.
7. Cubberley, Ellwood P. *Public School Administration*. Cambridge, MA: Houghton Mifflin Company, 1916.
8. Mann, Horace. "Seventh Annual Report of the Massachusetts Board of Education." Boston: Dutton and Wentworth, 1844.

9 Brownson, Orestes. "In Opposition to Centralization." *The Boston Quarterly Review*, 1839.
10 Mill, John Stuart. *On Liberty*. London: John W. Parker and Son, West Strand, 1859.
11 Mencken, H.L. "The Library: The Little Red Schoolhouse." *The American Mercury*, April 1924.
12 Mencken, H.L. "What Is Going On In The World." *The American Mercury*, February 1933.
13 US Census Bureau. "U.S. School Spending Per Pupil Increased for Fifth Consecutive Year." The United States Census Bureau, May 21, 2019. https://www.census.gov/newsroom/press-releases/2019/school-spending.html.
14 Dewey, John. "My Pedagogic Creed." *The School Journal* LIV (January 16, 1897): 77–80.
15 Kidd, Benjamin. *The Science of Power*. London: Metheun & Co. Ltd, 1918.
16 "Feasibility Study: Behavioral Science Teacher Educational Program." Washington D.C.: Michigan State University, 1969.
17 Sherman, Zander. *The Curiosity of School: Education And The Dark Side of Enlightenment*. Toronto: Viking, 2012.
18 Gates, Frederick Taylor. *Occasional Papers, No.1: The Country School of Tomorrow*. New York: The General Education Board, 1913.
19 Sirgany, Aleen. "The War On Waste." CBS News. CBS Interactive, January 29, 2002. https://www.cbsnews.com/news/the-war-on-waste/.
20 Ali, Idrees. "Pentagon Fails Its First-Ever Audit, Official

Says." Reuters. Thomson Reuters, November 15, 2018. https://www.reuters.com/article/us-usa-pentagon-audit/pentagon-fails-its-first-ever-audit-official-says-idUSKCN1NK2MC.
21 "Report to the Nations: 2018 Global Study on Occupational Fraud and Abuse." Association of Certified Fraud Examiners.
22 Peltier, Heidi. "The Cost of Debt-Financed War: Public Debt and Rising Interest for Post-9/11 War Spending." Brown University, January 2020. https://watson.brown.edu/costsofwar/files/cow/imce/papers/2020/Peltier 2020 - The Cost of Debt-financed War.pdf.
23 Rumsfeld, Donald H. September 18, 2002. http://www.sscnet.ucla.edu/polisci/faculty/trachtenberg/useur/rumsfeld180902.html.
24 Bush, George W. "President Bush Outlines Iraqi Threat." National Archives and Records Administration, October 7, 2002. https://georgewbush-whitehouse.archives.gov/news/releases/2002/10/20021007-8.html.
25 Lynch, Colum. "Document of the Week: The 2002 National Intelligence Estimate on WMDs in Iraq." Foreign Policy, August 9, 2019. https://foreignpolicy.com/2019/05/17/document-of-the-week-the-2002-national-intelligence-estimate-on-wmds-in-iraq/.
26 "Lawmakers Debate Action on Iraq." Cable News Network, October 9, 2002. https://www.cnn.com/2002/ALLPOLITICS/10/08/iraq.congress/index.html.
27 Bugliosi, Vincent. *The Prosecution of George W. Bush for Murder*. Vanguard Publications Incorporated, 2008.

28 Rycroft, Matthew. "The Secret Downing Street Memo." https://nsarchive2.gwu.edu/NSAEBB/NSAEBB328/II-Doc14.pdf

29 Wilson, Joseph C. "What I Didn't Find in Africa." The *New York Times*, July 6, 2003. https://www.nytimes.com/2003/07/06/opinion/what-i-didn-t-find-in-africa.html.

30 Hamburger, Tom, Peter Wallsten, and Bob Drogin. "French Told CIA of Bogus Intelligence." *Los Angeles Times*, December 11, 2005. https://www.latimes.com/archives/la-xpm-2005-dec-11-na-niger11-story.html.

31 Unger, Craig. "Craig Unger on Yellowcake Uranium." *Vanity Fair*, October 17, 2006. https://www.vanityfair.com/news/2006/07/yellowcake200607.

32 Suskind, Ron. "Faith, Certainty and the Presidency of George W. Bush." The *New York Times*, October 17, 2004. https://www.nytimes.com/2004/10/17/magazine/faith-certainty-and-the-presidency-of-george-w-bush.html.

33 Hitler, Adolf, 1889-1945. *Mein Kampf*. Boston: Houghton Mifflin, 1999.

34 Bernays, Edward L. *Propaganda*. New York: H. Liveright, 1928.

35 "Poison Ivy Lee and Propaganda." PR Academy, September 1, 2014. https://www.prplace.com/blog/posts/2014/september/poison-ivy-lee-and-propaganda/.

36 Dodd, Norman. The Special Committee Of The House of Representatives To Investigate Tax Exempt Foundations I (1954).

37 Wallace, Henry. "The Dangers of American Fascism." *New York Times*. April 9, 1944.

38 Gerrard, Howard, and Steve Zaloga. *Poland 1939: The Birth of Blitzkrieg*. Oxford: Osprey, 2003.
39 Lemnitzer, L.L. "Operation Northwoods." US Department of Defense. https://nsarchive2.gwu.edu/news/20010430/northwoods.pdf.
40 Ganz, James, and Eric Lipton. "A Search for Clues In Towers' Collapse; Engineers Volunteer to Examine Steel Debris Taken to Scrapyards." February 2, 2002. https://www.nytimes.com/2002/02/02/nyregion/search-for-clues-towers-collapse-engineers-volunteer-examine-steel-debris-taken.html.
41 "FEMA 403, World Trade Center Building Performance Study." FEMA, 2002.
42 "WTC Dust Signature Report Composition and Morphology." Damage Assessment 130 Liberty Street Property. RJ Lee Group Inc., December 2003. http://911research.wtc7.net/essays/thermite/cache/nyenvirolaw_WTCDustSignatureCompositionAndMorphology.pdf.
43 *Collateral Damages*. Turn of the Century, 2003.
44 "Collapse of Overpass in California Becomes Lesson in Construction." NewsHour, PBS, May 10, 2007.
45 Chang, Kenneth. "Scarred Steel Holds Clues, And Remedies." The *New York Times*, October 2, 2001. https://www.nytimes.com/2001/10/02/science/scarred-steel-holds-clues-and-remedies.html.
46 Jones, Steven E., et al. "Extremely High Temperatures During the World Trade Center Destruction." Journal of 9/11 Studies, February 7, 2008. Center Destruction."

Journal of 9/11 Studies, February 7, 2008. http://www.journalof911studies.com/articles/WTCHighTemp2.pdf.
47 "FBI Report: Dancing Israelis." Federal Bureau of Investigation. https://archive.org/details/DancingIsraelisFBIReport/page/n32/mode/2up.
48 "Statement Concerning SEC Terrorist Attack Trading Investigation." U.S. Securities and Exchange Commission, July 22, 2004. https://www.sec.gov/news/press/2004-98.htm.
49 Chesney, Marc, Remo Crameri, and Loriano Mancini. "Detecting Abnormal Trading Activities in Option Markets." *Journal of Empirical Finance* 33 (January 22, 2015). https://papers.ssrn.com/sol3/papers.cfm?abstract_id=1522157.
50 Winokur, Scott. "SEC Wants Data Sharing System / Network of Brokerages Would Help Trace Trades by Terrorists." *San Francisco Chronicle*, January 31, 2012. https://www.sfgate.com/business/article/SEC-wants-data-sharing-system-Network-of-2866659.php.
51 National Commission on Terrorist Attacks upon the United States. 2004. The 9/11 Commission Report: Final Report of the National Commission On Terrorist Attacks Upon the United States. New York: Norton.
52 "World Trade Center Disaster Seismic Observations." Lamont-Doherty Earth Observatory, Columbia University. https://www.ldeo.columbia.edu/LCSN/Eq/20010911_wtc.html.
53 Kennedy, John F. "REMARKS TO FLORIDA STATE CHAMBER OF COMMERCE." November 18, 1963.

54 Carcopino Jérôme, Henry T. Rowell, and E. O. Lorimer. ***Daily Life in Ancient Rome: The People and the City at the Height of the Empire***. Carcopino Press, 1941.
55 NY Penal Code §130.35
56 Rachel Sheffield, "The War on Poverty After 50 Years," September 15, 2014, https://www.heritage.org/poverty-and-inequality/report/the-war-poverty-after-50-years.
57 "Prison Spending in 2015." Vera Institute, n.d. https://www.vera.org/publications/price-of-prisons-2015-state-spending-trends/price-of-prisons-2015-state-spending-trends/price-of-prisons-2015-state-spending-trends-prison-spending.
58 McLaughlin, Michael, Carrie Pettus-Davis, Derek Brown, Chris Veeh, and Tanya Renn. "The Economic Burden of Incarceration in the U.S." Concordance Institute for Advancing Social Justice, 2016. https://joinnia.com/wp-content/uploads/2017/02/The-Economic-Burden-of-Incarceration-in-the-US-2016.pdf.
59 "Criminal Justice Facts." The Sentencing Project. https://www.sentencingproject.org/criminal-justice-facts/.
60 "Ancient History Sourcebook: Thucydides (C.460/455-C.399 BCE): Pericles' Funeral Oration from the Peloponnesian War (Book 2.34-46)." Internet History Sourcebooks. Fordham University. https://sourcebooks.fordham.edu/ancient/pericles-funeralspeech.asp.
61 Hess, Abigail J. "Average Tuition at Private Colleges Is $35,830 a Year-but Here's How Much Students

Actually Pay." CNBC, March 18, 2019. https://www.cnbc.com/2019/03/18/private-colleges-costs-35830-on-averagebut-students-may-pay-less.html.
62 Plutarch. *Life of Pyrrhus*.
63 Polybius. *The Histories.*
64 Chaffin, Tom. *Revolutionary Brothers: Thomas Jefferson, The Marquis De Lafayette, and The Friendship That Helped Forge Two Nations*. St. Martin's Press, 2019.
65 Claretie, Jules. *Camille Desmoulins and His Wife: Passages from the History of the Dantonists Founded Upon New and Hitherto Unpublished Documents*. Smith, Elder & Company, 1876.
66 "Napoleon Crowned Emperor." History, March 1, 2010. https://www.history.com/this-day-in-history/napoleon-crowned-emperor.
67 Englund, Will. *March 1917: On the Brink of War and Revolution*. W.W. Norton & Company.
68 Wheeler, John W. *Hindenburg in Twenty Years of German History, 1914-1934*. London: Archon Books.
69 Merridale, Catherine. *Lenin on the Train*. NY, NY: Picador/Metropolitan Books/Henry Holt and Company, 2017.
70 Crankshaw, Edward. "When Lenin Returned." The *Atlantic*. Atlantic Media Company, October 1, 1954. https://www.theatlantic.com/magazine/archive/1954/10/when-lenin-returned/303867/.
71 Lenin, Vladimir. *Selected Works*. Vol. 24. Moscow: Progress Publishers, 1970.

72 Figes, Orlando. *A People's Tragedy: A History of the Russian Revolution*. New York: Penguin Books, 1998.
73 Cicero, Marcus Tullius, Translated by M. T. Griffin, and E. M. Atkins. *On Duties*. Cambridge: Cambridge University Press, 2000.
74 Gasset José Ortega y. *The Revolt of the Masses: Translated from Spanish*. London: George Allen & Unwin, 1932.
75 Plato, Translated by G.M.A. Reeve, Revised by C.D.C. Grube. *Republic*.
76 Peter Viereck, Metapolitics: *The Roots of the Nazi Mind*, rev. ed. (1941; New York: Capricorn, 1965), 318.

Made in the USA
Columbia, SC
27 November 2020